THE THREE Ds OF DRAMA

(Dedication, discipline - and damned hard work)

First published in 1995

British Library Cataloguing in Publication Data
A catalogue record for this book is available from the British Library

ISBN 1 873295 90 1

Published and designed by Cross Publishing, Newport, Isle of Wight
Printed in Great Britain

THE THREE Ds OF DRAMA

By Dorothy Jamieson

Illustrations - James Hamilton
Foreword - Callum Mill

PUBLISHED BY CROSS PUBLISHING
NEWPORT, ISLE OF WIGHT

Also by Dorothy Jamieson

THE MEMORY BE GREEN published by Shetland Publishing Company 1988.
(The story of an incomer's life on the small island of Fetlar.)

To Grace Hamilton

and

Elsie Collier

As a member of Davidson's Mains Dramatic Club in Edinburgh, Dorothy Jamieson acted in and directed plays performed in the Little Theatre and later, the Church Hill Theatre.

A teacher in Trinity Academy Primary, she left to join the Drama Department. Later she became teacher in charge at the first Primary Drama Centre and then advisory teacher in Drama for the Lothian Regional Education Department.

Having attained an advanced diploma in speech and drama from the Central School (London) she went on to take a B.A. degree (O.U.) in Arts/Sociology.

Living now in Shetland she has adjudicated at one-act play festivals, directed a three-act play for Shetland, is a member of a sub-committee set up by the Arts Trust (Shetland) to consider the development of drama in Shetland and is now helping to run a new drama club on the island of Yell. Otherwise she lives a quiet life with her husband and their beloved cats.

CONTENTS

FOREWORD

In November I had a wonderful surprise: the manuscript of a book arrived from Yell in lovely Shetland from a friend I had not seen for some time - Dorothy Jamieson. The last time I remember was quite memorable. I shared the stage of the Little Theatre in Edinburgh with Dorothy and my future wife Nancy Forbes in Noel Coward's 'Present Laughter'. It was a short but very enjoyable run.

This quite unusual new book by Dorothy is directed at newcomers wishing to try their hand at 'acting' and later, perhaps, 'directing' within the ambience of an experienced and well-organised Amateur Dramatic Club. The writer deals with the initiation of one particular young lady and her problems with her first small part, in a very imaginative and quite unusual way. What is important is that she works from an actual script, making the problems and the solutions so much more realistic to the reader, who becomes totally involved with the actress in her involvement with her fellow actors, props, chairs and doors - and herself. The problems come alive and the solutions clarified.

The same clarity and charm, tinged with humour, runs through the struggles of the same young actress when she turns her hand to the quite different kind of problems the young 'director' meets preparing a One - Act play for a Festival.

We also learn what constitutes an Amateur Theatrical Club and how it is organised and financed - the operatives and the space they need.

Dorothy enjoys three distinct advantages in writing an informative book of this kind. First, there is her obvious love of the Theatre which shows through her writing. Second, there is her own specific dedication to the Amateur movement: she learned the kind of organisation it should be from her experiences as a member of one of the best-known and best organised Amateur Clubs in Edinburgh - the Davidson's Mains Dramatic Club: D.M.D.C. for short. Third, her experience as a Teacher which shows in the firm, clear, positive way of making her points - always tempered with a sense of enjoyment at another's success. She carefully catalogues the obstacles strewn in the way of a beginner, and then, in her inimitable way, based on hard-won experience and with a twinkle in her eye, leads the tenderfeet through the minefield. Averting disaster is the name of the game.

I enjoyed it thoroughly.

Callum Mill
Edinburgh, December 1994

INTRODUCTION

My purpose in writing this book is to support novices throughout their early months of working in a drama group. At the same time, I do hope that those who have 'been in it for years' will enjoy looking back to their own green beginnings when a hobby had not yet become a way of life.

That many of my friends were with me in spirit proved one of the pleasures of writing. Over years of involvement in amateur drama they shared with me the kind of experiences I talk about. To some of them I am grateful for advice, views and anecdotes, and to all of them for charmed and happy memories.

Occasionally our views on drama differed and they are in no way responsible for mine. We did agree, I believe, that there are countless ways-in to the study of acting and directing - that no one way is the 'correct' way. In advising my young beginner 'Bee' I kept this thought in mind, while pointing out that it's good to take account of well-tried precepts before branching out to try 'your own thing'.

My warm thanks are due to my life-long friends and fellow players Elsie Collier and Grace Hamilton for their encouragement and help with the 'nitty-gritty' of putting this book together. They never gave up hope that I'd stop talking about writing and sit myself down and do it!

Grateful to Albert Black for his generous advice and shrewd comments, my thanks extend to his wife Pat, who, though not 'in to' drama, bravely undertook to read the manuscript as if she were a beginner.

Albert is one of the three directors to whom I owe the strongly held belief on which this book is founded: that dedication, discipline and damned hard work are at the core of commitment to any worthwhile work in Theatre, be it professional or amateur. The two other directors are Callum Mill and the late George Cockburn.

I am indebted to Dr. Alan Ross and his wife Brenda, whose knowledge and experience of work backstage are phenomenal and who were with me in so many productions.

My thanks to Arthur Watt, the Arts Officer for Shetland, for his wise comments on drama and for giving me the opportunity to take drama workshops in Shetland.

To those who 'shared' theatre with me and in some cases wrote comments and observations, I am sincerely grateful. Amongst them were: Peter and Betty Black, Ivy Cluness, Gladys (Redpath) Cribbes, (fellow player and dear 'Props') Betty Horsburgh, who, sadly, died before the book's publication,

Catherine Hunter, Lorraine Jamieson, Helen Melville, who taught me so much about team work in comedy, Nancy (Forbes) Mill, Nan Murchison, Eric Burr....

Throughout this book I have tried to pass on to the beginner in drama that acting has little to do with solo performances - that one's best work is achieved through partnership - in team work - in liaison with backstage workers - in dedication to the ongoing production and - (if you're lucky) - in sharing the stage with gifted players.

I had that good fortune, and I salute here two players whose sensitive performances will long remain in the memory of D.M.D.C.'s audiences. I refer, of course, to Anthony (Tony) Harvey and the late Angus Spence.

Special love and thanks to the late Mildred E. Murray, M.B.E. who was a shining example of all that is best in drama to those who had the privilege of working with her in Davidson's Mains Dramatic Club.

My thoughts include others who are no longer with us though they live on in memory. Every one of them gave me something valuable, not only in dramatic insight but in friendship during the years we worked together and therefore gave of themselves to this book. I think, with love, of Allister Bryce, George Cockburn, Maisie Fairfoull, Betty Horsburgh, Reid Hunter, Ann Moar, Angus Spence and Dick Wanless.

My thanks to my husband James Jamieson, who knows all about working backstage and who, in partnership with Alan Ross, built so many beautiful sets throughout the years.

I am indebted to James Hamilton (the son of my friend Grace Hamilton) for his illustrations. His drawings, imbued with his own special brand of humour, have added another - and welcome - dimension to the book.

To Phil Mortimer a personal thank you for his help in demystifying the workings of my computer - and his great tolerance of my non-mechanical mind!

Finally, my grateful and very special thanks to Callum Mill for his kindness in writing the foreword to this book - to Scottish theatre lovers he was well-known as a professional actor of great distinction, and Edinburgh audiences will long remember his performances at the Lyceum Theatre, particularly as Bailie Nicol Jarvie in the Royal Command production of 'Rob Roy', as Vanya in Chekhov's 'Uncle Vanya' and his acclaimed interpretation of Willie Loman in 'The Death of a Salesman'.

Director of both the Citizens' Theatre Glasgow and the Traverse Theatre in Edinburgh at different times, he was, before this, a 'weel kent' S.C.D.A adviser, and to countless grateful Edinburgh amateurs, myself included, he was 'Callum' who taught us to take drama seriously and to treat acting with respect. I had the privilege of being directed by him on several occasions and learned a great deal of what I know about dedication, discipline, damned hard work - and love of theatre.

Following his years of beloved theatre work, he became a lecturer in Drama at Queen Margaret's College, Edinburgh, where he continued to inspire students through his teaching. On leaving Queen Margaret's he was awarded an honorary M.A.. A fitting close to a career for love of which he gave up his own opportunity to continue with University studies after the War.

If 'humility' had begun with the letter 'D' I would have included it in the book's title, for it is a quality integral to loving Theatre - and possessed in great measure by those whom I have mentioned here.

Dorothy Jamieson
Shetland, December 1994

CHARACTERS

In the book the reader will become acquainted with the following people:

BEE: (the name stands for Beginner):

(Although this character is a girl and the one to whom the letters are written, the advice on acting, directing and the setting up of a drama club applies equally to men and women.)

NARRATOR: Bee's guide and mentor - the writer of the letters and the notebook.

MRS MANNERS: An older 'lead' player in Bee's club.

SIMON: A young actor who shares in most of the happenings.

THE GROUP: Young members of the 'wee drama club' Bee and Simon help to set up - Pat, Anne, Joan, James, Mark and Andrew.

JANE: Bee's mother - friend of the narrator.

The Three Ds of Drama are:
Dedication, discipline and damned hard work.

PROLOGUE

NARRATOR'S NOTES:

I've just received a letter from my friend Jane's daughter. Having known Bee all her life it comes as no surprise that she wants to join a drama club - and from what Jane said on the phone today she seems 'mad keen'. She added: "It's all our fault - what can you expect when one's mother and her best friend's favourite topic of conversation is DRAMA!"

(Wonder what she means by 'fault'?)

Dear Bee,

Amateur drama as a hobby? You're not serious!

And yet you must be, for you've taken the first step by applying to join a club. Isn't it now a little late to ask me 'What were good to do?'

In any event Bee, as you are well aware, you turn to someone who, plunging into drama years ago, hasn't yet surfaced to ask whether it was a good idea. Perhaps before making a final decision you should weigh up a few pros and cons?

While you're practising lateral thinking, do consider the following: belonging to a drama club gobbles up spare time. Old friends? In despair they stop phoning you. Colleagues? They lunch with others, abandoning you to the company of a lonely sandwich and a playscript.

Last of all, you may find yourself viewed as slightly mad by those not in to drama. Why I heard of three total strangers who gave a wide berth to a drama club member. And this in the local park.

Does that puzzle you? If so, let me explain that my Thespian friend, while enjoying a dialogue with his labrador, wore the mental guise of Hamlet. The sight of him addressing his pet dog proved more than enough to make the passers-by exit from the scene.

Yet another player, although aware that arguing with Oberon while held up at traffic lights is - er - eccentric, was nonetheless affronted by the sight of motorists craning forward to hear better. Closing her car window she prayed that red would change to green. Quickly.

Snug on Titania's passenger seat a tape-recorder crackled forth the words of her beloved. That she had simply responded to these cues seemed beyond the perception of foolish eavesdroppers.

Has all this put you off? If so, dear Bee, you don't really intend to take up drama. Should you be serious then nothing anyone advises can hinder you from embarking on an exasperating, often irritating, always tiring way of life.
P.S. Entrancing of course.

NARRATOR'S NOTES:

...and why didn't I ask Bee whether she felt she had the ability to act? Why is this question rarely put to a would-be-member of a drama group?

"How do you know you can act?" Surely a simple thing to say? Isn't it?

Imagine a drama club room in which several people sit around a table pushed close to an ancient gas fire.

The president draws her chair nearer to the heat; having acted for many years there's little she doesn't know either about icy club rooms or amateur drama. Next to her sits the stage director who wouldn't be seen dead on the stage other than to organize settings. His word is *law* on scenery, painting, design and everything concerned with life backstage. To his right, shivering in a draught, huddles a committee member; she pokes a finger in all club pies. Opposite her, his chair tilted at a precarious angle, reclines the senior director, responsible for most club productions.

The secretary seated at the foot of the table, aware that her feet are freezing, wonders if she should make tea. The poor boy at her side looks as if he could do with a cup. 'The poor boy' is the would-be-member who has come for an interview with the committee.

PRESIDENT: *(She rustles some papers, none of which contains anything relevant to the interview in progress. Perhaps she feels it suits her role.)*
Now, Mr. - er - John - why did you say you wish to join this particular club?

WOULD-BE-MEMBER: Because *(he thinks this woman is mad)* because I want to act, so I thought I'd better apply to a - what you might call - top club. You know - with a good reputation.

(Silence, during which the committee think about the years of hard work it's taken to earn that reputation.)

DIRECTOR: *(hopefully)* Ah! Then you've had stage experience?

WOULD-BE-MEMBER: *(puzzled)* No - not yet. I'll get plenty of that with your group.

DIRECTOR: *(sadly, although he'd suspected it from the first)* I see.

(pause)

STAGE DIRECTOR: Are there other areas in which you've had exper... *(he looks over his specs at John)* - I mean, does anything else interest you other than acting?

WOULD-BE-MEMBER: What d'you mean? Well - what else *is* there?

STAGE DIRECTOR: Oh - backstage work, scene painting, lighting and - er - so on... *(his voice trails off)*

WOULD-BE-MEMBER: *(firmly)* I just want to *act.*

(a long pause)

SECRETARY: Yes - but - d'you suppose you could stretch that into doing a few mundane tasks - you know, join in day to day club life?

WOULD-BE-MEMBER: Yeah - sure! *(pause)* So long as I get to act.

PRESIDENT: *(hastily, as the legs of the Director's chair thump to floor level)* Yes, of course, Naturally. It's just that - well - we always work as a team -

COMMITTEE MEMBER: *(firmly)* What she means is that we all muck in with just about everything...

SECRETARY: and then some!

(they all laugh)

PRESIDENT: You can see we like our members to feel - committed.

WOULD-BE-MEMBER: Sure! That's O.K. by me.

PRESIDENT: *(She clears her throat. It's as telling as a pause.)* Right! *(She sneaks a glance at the Director who has his mouth open, presumably to speak.)* Now John, you do understand that at first we'd need to - let's say - start you off slowly - small parts...

DIRECTOR: In other words, you can't get a part right away - some teaching is necessary.

WOULD-BE-MEMBER: ....???

Dear Bee,

I send you the enclosed dialogue because it may help with the interview at your chosen drama club. I'll add a postscript as you may as well be aware of differing club policies before you take *your* plunge!

The P.S.

I stopped the scene at the moment when the W-B-M was about to utter. Why? Because no-one would believe that a W-B-M might not realize s/he would require teaching.

Mad, isn't it? After all, people joining a tennis club are aware that at the least they must whack the ball over the net before anyone's likely to breeze in with a "Who's for tennis?" And yet, Bee, a great many amateurs *do* believe that all they need do is learn lines, get up on stage, speak to the audience and "Magic! I'm an actor!"

Unfortunately there's no 'Heigh Presto' about it. Oh, I'm not discounting the fun of it all, but the pleasure is a by-product of dedication, discipline and damned hard work - the 3Ds of drama.

Would you say I've covered everything? The interview was searching, the committee spelled out the score and I've introduced you to the nitty-gritty in the above notes. So we've all done well! Or have we? Should the committee have said: "We're sorry, but acting isn't where your talents lie"? I think not; it was impossible for the committee to decide that, when the boy hadn't even had an audition.

On top of that, even with an audition, would-be-members are often so nervous that everyone rushes to give them the benefit of the doubt. When people have been accepted as members it becomes even more difficult to make such a statement.

What now? The answer depends on the club's philosophy. If their aims are improvement in standards of production and quality of acting, they must have a way of saying "Sorry, but No". A way that causes as little pain as possible.

Think about it yourself. Would it, for instance, be a workable idea to hold - not, as so often happens, a quick appraisal of actors saying a few lines - but the kind of audition which gives time for the nervous to steady themselves?

In the presence of the members, with everyone including the novice, taking part, a capable director could allow different kinds of play readings to be attempted in a relaxed atmosphere. At the same time, a few of the committee could act as discreet observers of the newcomer's abilities and at a private meeting, opinions could be voiced and decisions reached.

Something along these lines should be attempted. At least it's better than the inconsiderate way out taken by some committees, who, when they find new players don't have a clue about acting, simply stop giving them parts. Heartless.

A factor to bear in mind is: that you cannot TEACH people to act; the Director's words in the play were misleading. What he really meant was that beginners would be offered ways-in to acting by introducing them to

TECHNIQUES which help players come to grips with a character.

The beginners, while learning from BEING and DOING, absorb skills from those who know what they are about. All beginners? Sadly, for those without inner TALENT, no techniques, experience and practice exist, which are of value. Not in live theatre.

I'm not talking about *great* talent; a spark will do to light the way into a character's being, but without this skill, this art, the club's time and that of the audience is wasted.

What is shamefully worse is, that no amount of dedication, discipline and damned hard work can ever make up for the needless waste of a young person's time whose talents lie elsewhere.

NARRATOR'S NOTES:

I look forward with interest to hearing how Bee fared at her interview.

From my own knowledge of her, I think she'll do well. Though lacking a little confidence, she has a pleasant manner, a good speaking voice and carries herself well. These qualities count for something in drama, and belief in herself will follow. More importantly, if this club is as good as I've heard it is, the committee will give her time and opportunity to show whether or not she possesses the 'spark of talent'.

Must write and say that I'll certainly advise and encourage her through the months ahead. That's taking it for granted the club will accept her!

PART I

ALL ABOUT ACTING

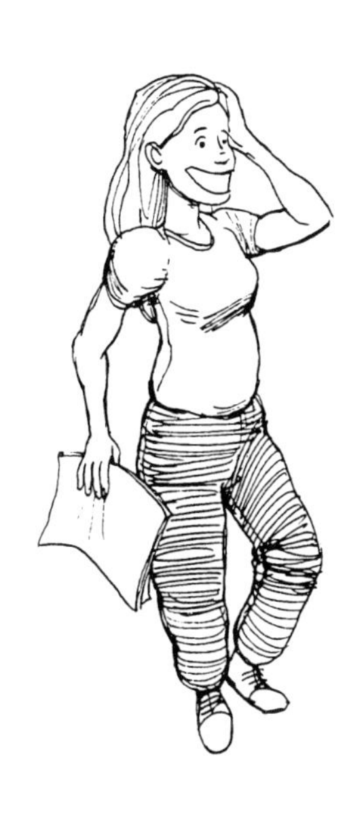

I

FIRST DAYS

(A. Bee as a novice)

Some weeks later: Bee has been accepted by a drama group:

Life in a drama club:

Dear Bee,

I get the feeling you're not looking forward to your first evening as a new member of the club, but although it's true that meeting strangers can be an ordeal, nervousness will only make your muscles tense up. Entering a room with a face like stone which says "No" to life, you'll spend the evening wondering why everyone looks as miserable as you.

Here's a piece of advice: before turning the door handle, take a deep breath. As you let it out, smile (even if it kills you) breathe "Yes", open the door and sail in.

Have fun!

NARRATOR'S NOTES:

Do hope things go well. Bee's reactions swither between excitement and an agony of self-doubt...

A day or two after the First Evening:

Dear Bee,

Good for you - the first hurdle safely jumped! Glad you enjoyed it. Never mind the initial dithering at the door - you got in with a "Yes". A tip to remember when you make an entrance on stage - yes?

How shrewd of the director to let you watch rehearsals. Make the most of it. Become invisible as you take everything in; you can materialize to help make tea. Should you wash up as well, approval will envelop you like a cloak.

Break-time, when players' voices become those of canaries set free from their cages, is the time to speak to people. In a few weeks the company will accept you as part of the scene and when the play begins to take shape, you'll soak up the atmosphere in which a creative project comes alive. Everything counts as experience.

Your description of the club room itself made me laugh. I agree that to take a cushion to pad the seat of your rickety chair would be excessive although there's nothing to stop you from piling on the woollies; keep warm and then your teeth won't chatter.

NARRATOR'S NOTES:

...memory hold the door! Bee's clubroom sounds just like the one I knew...

While the Club's plays were performed in town, rehearsals took place in a large hut in one of its suburbs. Nowadays, the Club own fine premises; they can't be as good as the hut.

Mind you, it was a venerable hut which had done service as a shoe-maker's premises. With thirty or more people crammed in, the floor boards complained audibly. In damp weather the door swelled up; the devil's own job to force open, it then required all one's strength to heave it shut.

Through myriads of nooks and crannies filtered sneaky currents of air busily turning noses blue on winter evenings. We took it in turn to dash in before rehearsal, switch on the electric fire (a danger to life and limb on the move) and coax the oil stove into life.

For the glory of being director of a play, the mighty paid the price by sitting in regal isolation opposite the draught from the door. Huddled in thick coats, gloved hands fumbled with notes while feet froze in their boots. At tea-break, the currently esteemed one moved like a zombie into the group round the fire; acting notes became noticeably crisp in November, thus allowing an earlier bee-line to the warmth.

Life felt better on all-day Sunday rehearsals. By seven o'clock the hot clammy air fought with cigarette smoke (not nowadays) while the orange curtains sagged with condensation. Though it doesn't sound better, we liked it that way. How we didn't develop pneumonia remains a wonder; certainly many of the cast sneezed their way through scenes while the pungent smell of cough sweets spiced the oil reek.

Memory contained in a hut chock full of friends, happiness and laughter. Silence too, broken by the rise and fall of players' voices interpreting a text, while in spirit they lived in the world of the Play.

We made a team and as a team, worked hard. Beginners took time to realize that no matter the occasional hilarity, we had one purpose: to bring a play to the theatre.

Two weeks later:

Bee's first part:

Dear Bee,

How sad that one of the cast became ill. How lucky that her part of the maid servant fell to you. "Just a tiny part," you wrote, "only a couple of lines."

Manna from heaven, Bee. In this way, as a member of a team, you may

stretch your wings with little stress. Don't be fooled, however, into thinking your part is unimportant just because you whisk 'on' and 'off'. Every actor appearing on stage contributes either to the play's success or failure.
P.S. A good thing you attended rehearsals. If you hadn't, the director might have forgotten your existence and some other girl wouldn't be able to sleep at night for thinking about it all.

NARRATOR'S NOTES:

...as for Bee, like a budding pianist practising the scales, it remains to be seen whether she can look forward not only to a few Chopin waltzes but a Beethoven sonata.

I wish her well.

Responsibility to audience:

Dear Bee,

You're so right in thinking you won't ever forget your first part on stage.

Yes, I do recall my own 'debut'! An effort of memory, for at the time I was the ripe old age of ten. About four of 'us bairns' wrote a play entitled 'THE TIMELY RESCUE'. Yes, one's first theatre venture is unforgettable.

As we played all the characters, you might suppose that dashing in and out of heroes', heroines', villains', old nurses' and a bishop's costumes was a trifle exhausting. You would be right.

NARRATOR'S NOTES:

Received a quick reply to my letter. Bee is fascinated by the idea that people she knows as adults could ever have been ten.

Dear Bee,

No, I don't have any photographs of The First Great Appearance! ...and yes, we did have an audience. Three performances we gave on that long ago Saturday in three houses in the neighbourhood. Although it's shameful to recall the first two shows, I'll force myself to do so because it's an excellent example of how *not* to treat your future audiences. Our only excuse, I suppose, for the bad behaviour was 'nerves'. We took refuge in squeals of laughter and when we forgot our lines we 'made it up'.

Not once did those polite audiences let us down. Smiling and applauding they seemed to enjoy every moment. Not for years did they confess their suffering. They were family.

In the third house we met with a different atmosphere. The audience of one, a lady who took life seriously, had accepted an invitation to see a play and see a play she would. Plump on a chair in front of the fireplace - our acting area - she regarded us with an air appallingly expectant. Not the teeniest of smiles twitched the muscles of her mouth.

"Come along, children," her whole body poured out messages, "entertain me."

Awed (not to say, terrified) respect for such an attitude killed our giggles stone-dead. I tell you, Bee, throughout my future life in drama I never concentrated more on the business of acting. Indeed the four of us brimmed over with determination to please. We gave the lady what every audience has the right to expect - our best performance.

II

EARLY REHEARSALS

Preparation:

Dear Bee,

Stay calm. Your first rehearsal will be the beginning of adventure!

Help appears on the page. Keeping in mind, however that you will have an adviser - in chief - your DIRECTOR - whose word is LAW, let's look at some suggestions you may find useful. I'll put them in 'list' form as they'll be easier to digest.

BEFORE YOUR FIRST REHEARSAL:

DO: read the play.

In rehearsal it's broken up into scenes and acts. Read it as a story and not only will you begin to sense the flow of the play but come to know the other characters' personalities.

DO: take a couple of pencils for writing into your script the moves the director gives you.

DO: make a quick drawing of the set. You'll probably find that the stage manager has pinned one on the notice board. If not - ask!

DO: note where doors, windows and furniture are placed. A plan is handy when you're working at home.

AT THE FIRST REHEARSAL:

DO: write your moves in clearly as a scribble means you can't decipher them.

Take your time. Write *all* your moves. The director won't give a prize for being finished first. In any event it's better to keep a cast waiting now, than to infuriate them later because you've failed to write in essential instructions.

DO: attend to the director's NOTES. They are given more to help you than to criticise.

DO: listen to everyone's notes. Not only will they be useful to your own part but you'll learn a great deal about production and see the play as a WHOLE.

Even though it's early days you can't begin too soon to think of yourself as a member of a TEAM.

NARRATOR'S NOTES:

...must keep on emphasising the need to think of TEAM. Some players get themselves into a kind of ecstatic vacuum which is self-defeating. Absorbing the 3Ds of drama includes an understanding of relationships.

Forgot to thank her for the copy of her play script. We'll find it useful.

The script:

(The scene is the drawing room of a large country house.
Time: the summer of 1890.
Through the large windows to left of stage can be seen a garden with trees. Centre right is a door leading to the hall. The room is comfortably furnished with deep armchairs, a sofa and little tables. In front of the window is a table set for tea.)

Seated to the left of table is Mrs. Manners (a well-to-do widow who owns the house). She is speaking to an elderly gentleman seated to right of table. An old friend of her late husband's, he is the local squire.

MRS. MANNERS: *(pouring tea into cups)* ...and what will be the outcome of all this I really cannot imagine. *(She hands a cup and saucer to the squire.)*

SQUIRE: Thank you. *(He settles back in his chair.)*
Yes - I can appreciate the difficulties. *(He stirs his tea thoughtfully.)* May I ask what Emily's - er - reaction is to Ronald's behaviour?

MRS. MANNERS: *(ruefully)* You know Emily! *(The squire smiles.)* She informed me that... *(she breaks off as the door opens)*

Enter Mary, a young maid servant. (She carries a small cake stand. Closing the door, she crosses left to the table at the window. Placing stand on table she moves slightly above and to the right of Mrs. Manners.)

MARY: *(curtseys)*: Please ma'am, Miss Emily says to tell you that she has a headache and won't be down to tea.

(pause)

MRS. MANNERS: I see. Thank you Mary. You may go.

MARY: Yes ma'am. Thank you ma'am. *(She crosses the stage to the door.)*

MRS. MANNERS: Wait! Mary!

MARY: *(turns)* Yes ma'am?

MRS. MANNERS: You may tell Miss Emily that Mr. Ronald will be here in half an hour.

MARY: Yes ma'am. Of course ma'am. *(She exits.)*

Marking in lines

Dear Bee,

Many players find it helpful when learning their lines, to mark, in some way, the words their character has to speak. They feel that by doing this, the lines stand out more clearly. There is a lot to be said for it as long as it doesn't lead the player into ignoring the lines of the other characters.

Various methods are used: some players underline all the lines they have to say. Some underline the last words of their partner (their cues). Some go so far as to shade in their dialogue with a coloured pencil. Some mark only the words which they wish to stress - and so on.

Using red ink, some players also mark in their cues for exits and entrances (excellent!)

Those who like to go to a lot of trouble, gum sheets of blank paper in between each page of the script, and on this write all the moves, directions etc. that the director has given them. As well, they number each line of the printed script and on the blank sheet write e.g. Line 6 X to ch. 2 (cross to chair 2) and so on. (The advantage here is that they can be more expansive with their notes.)

Most players, however, underline their speeches and write abbreviated instructions in the margin. N.B. Whatever you choose, it's safer to use a pencil rather than a pen. It has been known for a director to change instructions!

Entrances and exits - introduction to:

Dear Bee,

That you fell asleep in bed while reading over the director's notes doesn't surprise me: rehearsals are exhausting and a lot of nervous energy goes into acting. In your letter you mention your ENTRANCE as Mary. My apologies for not including a note about this - and EXIT - in our list.

You say the director criticized your entrance. He was probably pointing out the necessity of VISUALIZING the door. Obviously the door will be in place at performance. In rehearsal you must imagine that the space chalked out by the stage manager is a large wooden door! The best way to do this is to MIME opening and closing it.

Now: from your sketch I see that the door opens ON STAGE i.e. away from you as you go in. Check whether it opens to the left or to the right and then push it. When the time comes to EXIT pull it towards you - it's amazing just how many players forget whether they must pull or push the door i.e. if they hope to get out.

Unforgettable is the player who struggled to exit via a door which opened OFF STAGE by pulling it towards her - ON STAGE. Finally, she gave it such an almighty heave that the canvas door swayed towards her like a sail capsizing. At this (late) point she came to her senses, managed to push the flat upright again, open the door the correct way and make her - escape.

Remember: every time you either go ON or OFF stage at rehearsal, MIME opening and closing the imagined door.

NARRATOR'S NOTES:

Don't think this is the time to tell Bee what happened next to my suffering player: the reality of the play destroyed, the audience, apart from the director (who probably fainted) had to recover from their hysterical mirth. Indeed, they never quite did so. Till the end of the play a muffled squeak arose at intervals from the auditorium as one individual after another succumbed to the memory of a player battling with the scenery.

FIRST ENTRANCE:

Dear Bee,

You say that your director keeps reminding the cast that entrances, particularly FIRST entrances, are important. This is because audiences appreciate seeing a 'new' face. Nerve racking though it is, every eye focuses upon you. And why not? That's why you are there.

Whisper "Yes" with purpose, pause for a scrinch of a second, enter and close the door firmly (if that is a given move) *know* why you are there and *get on with it.*

Later, we'll talk about the TIMING of your entrance and exit.

NARRATOR'S NOTES:

There's little use in speaking in depth about 'timing' entrances and exits at this point in rehearsals because Bee says she's still reading from her script.

All the same, it'll be interesting to see when she becomes aware of the need to time them herself.

LATE ENTRANCE: (Bee wrote to tell me that the lead player was "not pleased with me".)

Dear Bee,

Mrs. Manners might have been wiser to let the director tell you that you were late on your entrance. She does have a point though! She's the one waiting for you! Let's see if we can work out where you went wrong.

Look at your script:

Not at the line which says 'Enter Mary'.

Not at your CUE LINE i.e. Mrs. Manners' line - You know Emily! She informed me that... - (She breaks off because the door opens.)

Look *first* at the squire's line about Emily's reaction to Ronald's behaviour. This is when *you must put your hand on the door knob.* If you only start getting ready on -She informed me that... - (your cue line) you will be late on entrance. PUSH the door open on -You know Emily- or before you've got yourself on stage Mrs. Manners will have finished her line. Poor soul, she has to break off when she sees you. If you are LATE she's left either with nothing to say or having to AD LIB (make it up!)

Concentrate on TIMING your entrance so that you are on stage when Mrs. Manners needs you. Team work required here.

NARRATOR'S NOTES:

Oh for performances where everything comes off perfectly. Damned hard work helps, for it's just luck when things sketchily rehearsed 'go right on the night'. The unjust factor remains that *one* actor's mistake can affect everyone on stage.

Bee found that when she muffed her entrance not only did she spoil her own first appearance but Mrs. Manners also became involved in the agony. Why? Because *nothing* on stage happens in isolation - every player is part of the action. (Perhaps in a monologue an actor might consider him/herself alone!)

In a perfect world no players could say either "I've never appeared in a play where an entrance went wrong" or "I've never made a poor entrance". Ha!

Dear Bee,

Am so glad you've tussled your way through that problem. Entrances are the very devil and the sooner you take them as seriously as you take your lines, the smoother life in drama will be - for everyone concerned.

Yes, you may well wonder what would happen if a player didn't appear at all! A nightmare thought - and the reality strikes terror into the hearts of all on stage. Make no mistake - it can happen - I've seen it.

It's not that the player due on stage didn't come on but he arrived such a *long* time after the cue had been given - and given - and given, that those on stage thought he'd got lost.

The play was well into the third act and no-one expected a disruption to the calm. Two players, a man and a girl stood together on stage. Their romantic duologue over, the actor gave the cue for a third player to enter. No-one came. Pause. The actor repeated the cue line. No-one appeared. Perspiring under his make-up, he ad-libbed, striving to keep to the spirit of the scene. The girl and he shook from head to toe. Hand in hand they encouraged each other to speak a few lines. Bravely and indeed expertly, they played their parts. Still no-one came.

The prompter searched for an aspirin; the stage manager issued frantic instructions to stage crew to "find him!" and again whispered fiercely into the dressing room intercom.. Meanwhile the director seated in the packed theatre closed his eyes and wished he was home with a good book.

On stage, the actor glared at the door and in hollow tones, quoth, "Perhaps - perhaps something has happened to..."

On to the stage erupted the latecomer. Red-faced with embarrassment, he blustered his way into the scene. Played by three frightened people it took effort to recapture the flow of the scene. Not one member of the company had escaped suffering. Now, the director cautiously opened his eyes and relaxed trembling in his seat, the back-stage team remembered how to breathe and the prompter put the aspirin back in its bottle. Normality returned - at a cost.

That, Bee, is what might happen if you didn't appear. Would you like to know the end of the story?

Epilogue:

SCENE: Men's dressing room.

CHARACTERS: The Actor, Stage Manager, Director and CULPRIT.

The culprit is seated at the dressing table as the three Indignants fling open the door and crowd into the room.

The Director glowers. (As the culprit is a dearly loved and talented player he hesitates to begin.) The Stage Manager leans against the door. (To prevent an escape?)

DIRECTOR:	*(sternly)* Well? What happened to you?
STAGE MANAGER:	*(virtuously)* You were called in time.
CULPRIT:	*(sadly)* I'm sorry. Really very sorry.
	(pause)
ACTOR:	*(astounded)* Is that all? What *happened?*
	(pause)
CULPRIT:	I couldn't find my braces.

III

REHEARSALS CONTINUE

Without script:

Dear Bee,

By all means do without the script. The moment you feel sure of your lines, *when* you say them and know all the moves the director has given you, is the time to rehearse without it.

Only now are you free to deal with the imaginary door, move with purpose and instead of mumbling into your book, speak with your head straight. Not only may you communicate with the other players but how grateful they'll be to see your eyes.

NARRATOR'S NOTES:

Bee should start to enjoy the rehearsals now. She's been so worried about the mechanics of moving she's not had opportunity to think of her part as Mary.

Dress for rehearsals:

Dear Bee,

A Victorian maid servant in a 20th century mini skirt? - find a long skirt for rehearsals!

Yes, it matters. As you won't see your stage costume till the dress rehearsal, at least get the 'feel' of the part by wearing a long sleeved blouse, a mob cap (improvise with a large handkerchief) apron and appropriate shoes. With these and a long skirt, not only will you gain the spirit of the period but invaluable help with the character.

What about your hair? Practise tucking it into your cap - club finances may not stretch to the hiring of wigs for the smaller parts. How lucky that your hair is long - which reminds me of O.C.D. (our chief director!) who used to say, "Every actress worth her salt should let her hair grow." And to actors? "Get it cut!"

NARRATOR'S NOTES:

Bee responded by asking (dramatically) "Surely it's the soul, personality - what ever you like to call it - of Mary - that's of first importance?"

Quite right! Having agreed with her, I hope she'll still see the necessity of wearing, even at rehearsals, clothes which help to build the character of Mary rather than hinder its birth.

Dear Bee,

So pleased that you felt more like Mary when you tried out a long skirt etc.

You ask what the most important thing is to do now. EVERYTHING you do from the time you come into view on stage is important, although life becomes easier once you're in character.

Think about this: through time you, like all players, will find your own ways-in to interpreting character. In the meantime, there's no harm in getting to know some well-tried methods before deciding to ignore them in the light of your own experience.

Questioning your character is one procedure:

e.g. What's my purpose in this play?
Where is Mrs. Manners' house - in town or in the country?
As we know it's in the country - am I a local girl?
Do I live in the village - or what?
Is Mrs. Manners a kind employer?
Will her attitude to me make any difference to my behaviour?
You don't get much help from the script - apart from being told that you come in!
Let's find some clues:
As Mary, are you thinking about Emily when you enter?
Do you know why she won't come down to tea?
Do you feel sorry for her - or what?
Are you interested in Mrs. Manners' reaction to Emily's message? Did you notice that she doesn't ask about poor Emily's headache?
Are you disappointed Mrs. Manners simply tells you to go?
Do you realize what the message about Ronald will mean to Emily?
Do you care?
Are you going to go to Emily straight away?

(...and you can think up dozens more yourself.) BUILD Mary with tiny bricks of imagination until she becomes real to you.

Don't be carried away by all this. These questions are only to help you feel that *you* are Mary. On your exit, Mary's part is over. Don't mislead the audience into thinking that she's important to the play's development.

What does that mean? It means: Don't draw attention to yourself in any way that would spoil the balance of the story; the audience are interested mainly in Mrs. Manners' reactions - you are there to help bring that about. Besides which: you'll upset the director.

NARRATOR'S NOTES:

Stage stealing:

The truth is that players can, on occasion, take away from another's performance; lack of experience causes them to give their all in a way harmful to the POINT OF THE SCENE. For those players who do such a thing deliberately, no excuse holds good.

Difficult to fight back, it isn't impossible, for when they are riled, experienced players can give as good as they get. Two evils don't put matters right; while players fight verbally to gain the upper hand, not only are they harming the play but the expectations of their long-suffering audience.

Dear Bee,

You're correct! Spoiling the balance is a polite phrase for stage stealing!

The best way to deal with it, I think, is to hold on to your temper when someone does it to you. Leave it to the director to say a few well-chosen words in the ear of the baddie.

Yes, I do recall a gruesomely unforgettable occasion when this happened:

Two lessons - learned by a young lass during a tiny appearance in a play set in the 18th century. The part: that of a maid in a scene with her employer. (Just like you!)

The mistress is knitting. On a stool beside her sits the maid, winding a ball of wool. The maid has little to do apart from supplying interested reaction to her mistress's words.

On the first night all goes well. Paralysed inwardly with fright, the maid hardly moves, except to wind wool in the intervals when attention is supposed to be on her.

A newspaper report describes this scene as one of the best things in the play. Such rapture, Bee! Mentioned in a theatre crit.! Never mind that her name didn't appear, nor indeed was her acting under discussion. She felt of tremendous importance.

That night on stage the maid relaxed (and jubilant) pays little or no attention to her partner. Instead she busies herself with the work box on her knees. My goodness! What a muddle! Painstakingly (and with many a sigh) she whisks the threads into neat balls. Oh, the joy of it.

All good things must end. Her exit line arrives; putting down the box, she prances off-stage.

In the sea-gloom of the wings, a long arm stretches out, drawing the wee maid forward. The arm belongs to the director. His usually jovial face fixed in a scowl, he seems an odd purplish colour; perhaps it's a trick of the lighting.

He breathes wheezily. "Lassie," he whispers, "as long as you live, never, *never* do that again!"

"Do what?" stutters the ignorant lass.

"Don't ever steal a scene from another player or -"

He never finishes the sentence as, from the stage, comes the maid's cue for re-entrance. With a blood-curdling scream, she careers on stage. The scream, thankfully, is part of the play.

After the performance, the director came up to her. "Lassie," he said, "I apologise. Mind, you were wrong in what you did and I'm not taking it back. But I wouldn't have spoken to you then, if I'd remembered you were due on stage." He sighed gloomily. "Well, you're a sensible lass and I guess you'll not stage steal again. What's more," his eyes laughed, "I'll wager that however long you act, you'll never give a better screech than you did to-night!"

In his first belief he was correct. The wee lassie learned a lesson for which she thanks in memory, a wise and kindly director; never consciously, from that night, did she take a scene away from another player.

He was wrong about the second. On the rare occasions screaming was called for in a play, she managed fine. She only had to recall the director's voice whispering truths in her ear, for her to guarantee the audience a truly awesome screech.

NARRATOR'S NOTES:

Not long till Bee goes to the theatre. She'll find that now's the time a wee bit of tension creeps into rehearsals as the director asks for even more from his cast. Bee is determined to get everything right.

Timing moves:

Dear Bee,

Let's give the director the benefit of the doubt! When he said, "Get moving!" he was probably asking you to think about where you should be on any given line.

e.g.: After Mrs. Manners' line, you move smoothly to the table (short steps - you're in Victorian dress).

You don't start your line about Emily till you've moved right of Mrs. Manners.

On her answer, you curtsey and "Get Moving" to the door.

Mrs. Manners' call -Mary-, stops you in your tracks and you TURN towards her.

After her instructions, you turn again, move to the door, hand on door knob and EXIT, closing the door quietly.

The secret of neat movement on stage is to get your feet going so that *you finish the move as you finish speaking.*

This means that on short lines you start walking just *before you speak.*

When you have a long line on a short move, speak a few words *before you move.*

Using these techniques ensures you don't have lines still to say which would have 'come over' better while on the move. (A director helps with these.)

Although some of these remarks don't apply to Mary, they are worth remembering for future performances. In the meantime, *watch* how players with bigger parts cope with moves.

NARRATOR'S NOTES:

Pre-dress rehearsal:

Bee's dress rehearsal is upon us! I shan't worry her with too much advice at this stage. As long as she gets through the performances, giving her best all the time, she'll do.

Dear Bee,

The 'butterflies' in your tummy are twinges of nervousness. Mrs. Manners is perhaps right in saying this proves you are an imaginative actor.

Although fine as far as it goes, just make sure you don't allow excitement to rule your life. Acting isn't just 'feeling'; concentrate on things which encourage a calm approach to problems.

Put it this way: you won't be any less of an imaginative actor if you remember to take all that you need to the theatre and pack your case properly!

On dress rehearsal night, leave for the theatre full of expectation at the thought of the hours ahead. (It's too late now to keep rehearsing the part in your mind. You can do nothing valuable until you face real live characters on stage.)

NARRATOR'S NOTES:

Bee is lucky in that she has two rehearsals in the theatre: a practical one, which for the players means a chance to concentrate on the mechanics of moves and get used to the set.

For the backstage team it means concentrating on lighting and rehearsing scene changes.

The following night is the dress rehearsal itself.

IV

IN THE THEATRE

Atmosphere:

Dear Bee,

Delighted that you enjoyed the first rehearsal. As you say, theatre atmosphere is a quite unexpected bonus and almost impossible to explain. As soon as players go through the stage door something magical happens. Everyday worries slip away in a world where everyone's thoughts concentrate on one thing only - performance.

Tomorrow you'll feel happy to be a part of this world as you prepare to go on stage.

NARRATOR'S NOTES:

Theatre! Its enchantment takes hold from the moment players push open the stage door. Running upstairs they may pause by the opening into the stage wings. From here comes the sound of hammering mingled with the cheerful shouts of stage crew calling to each other. The air is heavy with the sharp scent of paint, glue size, canvas and furniture polish.

On into the women's dressing room, where the lights over the mirrored walls blaze on the faces of the women seated before them, putting on stage make-up. Comforting low-key chattering in the background as everywhere dart the wardrobe mistress and her team, shaking out costumes, helping players into them and hanging up garments needed later. A team at work with every member knowing her part.

The men's dressing room seems on a different planet. Not for them the gossip and the giggles; here a decent reverent hush prevails. The players regard themselves in the glass as if wondering how they've got there; conversation limits itself to the tasks in hand. Not till the first coffee break do the men relax. The agony of struggling into costumes finished with, rehearsal of the first act behind them, they join in the general chatter.

Whether performance takes place in a well-equipped playhouse such as the one Bee finds herself in, a village hall, barn or ramshackle hut, the atmosphere of theatre is always present. You can almost touch it. It's there in the heightened excitement, in the hub-bub of backstage, on the newly set stage and in the quiet depths of the auditorium where the director watches his production struggle into life. 'Rough magic' is abroad.

Fortunate Bee!

Later:

Dress rehearsal:

The cast were allowed to invite a few guests to the dress rehearsal. Bee duly asked me to go with Jane her mother.

"Woe is me and all that lark!" as Bee would say. Jane and I didn't know whether to laugh or cry. However, after several cups of coffee and long discussion after the performance I gave her a note to hand to Bee when she got home.

Hazards with properties:

Dear Bee,

Let me say first how much I enjoyed the rehearsal. Despite the catastrophe (which we'll discuss) you did well indeed.

To begin at the beginning:

As Mary, you opened the door (which seemed a little stiff) so you gave it an extra push (sensible).

Unfortunately the door jerked slightly and in sight of the audience, two cakes slid off the cake stand in your left hand.

The scene then went something like this:

First, a somewhat tense pause during which Mary looked stricken and Mrs. Manners, astounded, as they both watched the little round cakes bounce across the stage.

As the director instructed the cast to "play it for real" you had to continue:

MRS. MANNERS: *(clearing her throat)* Ah! It's you Mary! Never mind the cakes - accidents will happen. Come here and put the stand on the table.

MARY: *(gratefully)* Thank you ma'am. Sorry ma'am.

The scene then continued 'as book' till Mary turned to walk back across stage. She was now wondering what to do about the cakes.

Beside me, your mother leant forward in her seat and (fortunately in a whisper) said, "For heaven's sake Bee - pick 'em up - pick 'em up!" Mary picked them up! (Hurray! Hurrah!) Meantime Mrs. Manners waited till Mary started to get up before speaking.

There's no doubt that this player's experience and presence of mind helped the day. Her remarks were an example of ad-libbing at its best because at the same time she made sure that you received help.

Nonetheless, if you had gone to pieces and failed to respond, the scene would have been ruined. Take heart from that and be glad that in a crisis you came through on discipline and team work!

Could these things have been prevented from happening in the first place?

Think of the 'stiff' door. Made of painted canvas with a wooden frame, for whatever reason, it stuck.

Certainly the stage manager should have been aware of this and too, so should the cast; they all came on stage through it. Don't worry. That's what rehearsals are for and it will be put right before tomorrow.

Those blessed cakes! All articles used in a play are known as properties and the person in charge of these is the Property Mistress. It was up to her to make sure that they wouldn't slide off at the 'practical' rehearsal the previous night. On the other hand, are *you* entirely blameless? Ask yourself: "Did I rehearse in the club room or at the first theatre rehearsal with *real* properties or did I make do with imagining them?"

It is your right to insist on practising with real props or efficient stand-ins. O.K., you're inexperienced but I expect you'll make sure that it doesn't happen again!

Put all these things out of your mind meantime and *enjoy* your first night, safe in the knowledge that you can cope.

NARRATOR'S NOTES:

Stage business:

Bee found out the hard way that things seem to bounce up and hit her which, amongst all the worries that haunted her, she'd never dreamed of. Heavens above! That's almost a literal thought!

Troubles often pop up where stage business is concerned.

N.B. Explain to Bee, once the play is over, about coping with lines and properties at the same time.

Meantime I'm looking forward to the performance on Saturday night.

Performance:
After seeing the final night's performance:
Dear Bee,

Congratulations on a production which the audience thoroughly enjoyed.

You did well indeed: you looked right, you were believable and furthermore, every word rang crystal clear. "Yes" in answer to your next question - you showed a great deal of promise.

How fortunate to have joined such a good team.

NARRATOR'S NOTES:

...can't expect Bee to understand the full scope of the word 'team' - Director, stage director, stage manager, committee, players, stage crew, property mistress, wardrobe mistress and helpers, lighting group, prompter, call boys, effects team, business manager, front-of-house team and so many others... each one an integral part of performance.

...if not cast in the next play, hope Bee decides to work, in some capacity, back-stage. Not only will she enjoy theatre without the trauma of going on stage, but she'll appreciate production from another angle.

(O Wise Back-stagers who see more of the game than unsuspecting players realize!)

POSTSCRIPT

Properties - again!
Dear Bee,

After all the excitement of last week, plus the end of show party you must, as you say, be feeling a bit flat. Never mind, there'll be more plays to come.

You reminded me to talk about properties: I'll start by saying that using properties on stage is part of what's known as STAGE BUSINESS. (May I add that that forms a great deal of 'the damned hard work of drama' i.e. juggling with lines and things to do, at the same time.)

Though it's true you should always rehearse with the correct props, I think I was a bit hard on you. What I didn't say was, that although some errors can be blamed happily on either the property team or the carelessness of the player involved, it's a fact of life that mistakes turn up no matter how careful the preparation.

Sometimes properties break in one's hand. An experienced player I knew had recurring nightmares about papier mâché vases. No wonder, for in a never-to-be-forgotten one-act play festival, one papier mâché vase after another broke in her hands.

The back stage crew ran out of spares; when, in desperation, she fled off stage to find something - anything - that resembled a vase, they handed her the one they'd decided not to use and it too fell apart as she entered.

Some properties aren't on stage at all; some are on stage when they shouldn't appear till the next act; some don't function; some lie snug in a cupboard next to the one in which the player frantically searches and any one of these mishaps can make lines fly out of players' heads.

Some props have a dire effect on individual players: phone calls on stage and even worse, pouring out drinks. Many players can't even bear to think of making a bed on stage. The effort of flapping sheets about while trying to remember lines is something they'd rather forget.

On one occasion a player was preparing to set a table when the drawer which held the cutlery, jammed. Her mind froze at the thought of the players coming on to eat, with only their fingers to pick up food. Fortunately her stage son pushed her on one side and the drawer slid open for him.

Another player shuddered at the idea of wearing a sword. This little hate dated from the time he couldn't haul one out of its scabbard.... One day Bee, you'll have your own list of pet hates. Take comfort from the fact that players continue to act despite their 'hate' relationship with some props. Either it says much for their love of theatre or that they just like suffering!

V

A BIGGER PART

(B. Bee learns more)

Bee's club have chosen their Spring play - a light, sophisticated comedy.

Being 'natural':

Dear Bee,

So pleased you've been cast; Julia, the daughter sounds a satisfying part, and that you have one really 'meaty' scene, is great news.

You write: "I shan't, thank goodness, need to bother about movement. As it's a modern play I can just act naturally."

The blithe assumptions you make! In the first place you will always have to bother about movement on stage. That the play is a present-day comedy certainly means that costume will be easier to wear than the petticoats of Victorian times. Movement, however, belongs to the character portrayed and not to you! It *must* be given thought; everything on stage is premeditated, all is rehearsed, including bothersome movement.

Bee dear, my mind has gone blank. Come to tea.

NARRATOR'S NOTES: (a week later)

...and I'm not convinced that Bee returned home with any changed views on not bothering. She believes that as long as she learns her lines intelligently, that's all there is to it.

Dear Bee,

Let me tell you about O.C.D. (you remember? - Our Chief Director).

He was the first one to instil in us the importance of movement on stage. Oddly, not so much from what he said, for he rarely put into words his deep feelings on the subject; it's difficult to recall him even showing players what was wrong with the way they moved.

On the other hand, as we walked across the rehearsal area, his face, glooming from the side-lines, signalled that he expected more from us. When, however, we glimpsed even the teeniest of smiles beginning a slow journey across his face, the warm glow that reached out to us, eased tension; from that moment we tripped across stage bathed in approval.

Whatever O.C.D.'S secret, it had something to do with the belief that radiated from him that you had, at last, found your character.

Do you know, such was the awed respect we had for him, that during one rehearsal a very young player confided as we made tea in the back kitchen that she had had a "frightening dream last night."

"O.C.D." she whispered, glancing nervously at the open door, "glued my hands to the stage."

Although we giggled about this, she went on, "It wasn't really funny. I had the nightmare after last night's rehearsal." She tiptoed to the door and closed it. "You know how he's always whispering to the prompter?" I nodded. O.C.D. preferred to share any dismal views with an assistant stage manager rather than burden players with them!

"Well, his face got sort of thundery and he muttered away about 'people (meaning me) flapping their arms about like demented seagulls!'" She sighed. "He's good on the animal kingdom, isn't he?"

Together we reflected on clumsy elephants, timid mice, waddling penguins... O.C.D.'s (meant to be) private list was endless. We burst out laughing and went back refreshed into the rehearsal room.

I may add that during the rehearsal she stopped fluttering her hands aimlessly (an everyday habit of hers) and gave a thoughtful performance.

NARRATOR'S NOTES:

...not that Bee isn't prepared to give all her attention to studying her part. She nods her head in agreement to that; where I lose her is in the thick haze of faulty ideas she peers through when it comes to thinking of character in terms of movement. Her attitude is "I can walk and as nobody's ever said I'm disagreeable to look at, let's take all that for granted and get on with the lines".

It's a pity she never met O.C.D..

...of course she can take her first two statements for granted. It isn't enough, however, to concentrate solely on dialogue; her part is not in a play for Radio. Even if it were, Radio actors do visualize each character complete with body, gestures and mannerisms.

Including the body:

Dear Bee,

How I wish I'd known O.C.D. in my very much younger days. Most of my problems would have melted away if I'd realized just how important it is to include the body as a part of character building.

Nervousness, for example, makes muscles seize up and it's useless to try to ignore a tensed-up body which must be relaxed and flexible enough to ask of it anything needful.

The body speaks a language of its own. (Remember the lady who saw me as a child in my first play? Her whole body 'poured out messages' without her saying *one word.*)

The next time you're in a restaurant take a look at the people sitting around you. There's a lot you can tell about other people from their appearance, age, mannerisms, gestures and facial expressions. And all this without hearing one word they are saying!

To an extent, the key to building a stage character is in understanding body language. Then and only then will you be able either to make use of your own gestures and movements, or discard those not suitable for the part.

It follows, that the enemies of trying to get into the skin of your character are nervousness and tension in your own body. So don't just rely on understanding the character's mind, however sensitive that may be, for it isn't possible to COMMUNICATE the personality and finer feelings of the character to an audience if your body is either too stiff to respond, or you ignore the character's body as central to interpretation.

Dear Bee,

I would like you to concentrate on the idea of:

Moving in character:

As your rehearsals don't start for another week, let's spend the time in talking about this.

You already know that the director will be responsible for your MOVES and obviously, *where* you are when you say your lines is of great importance to you, to your fellow players - and to *the point of the scene.*

Of equal importance is what you *do.* Some of these tasks will be given by the director; he may wish you for instance: to open a drawer (!) close the curtains, lift the telephone and so on at specific points in the play. You may have lines to say at the same time. This, as we've talked about, is STAGE BUSINESS.

Of even greater importance in getting into your part are the things which *you* in the main will be responsible for, such as gestures and movements which are part of your character's personality e.g. *How* Julia opens a drawer!

Gesture:

At all times on stage keep in mind that the audience, apart from LISTENING to you, are WATCHING a MOVING picture; the director is in charge of changes in the rhythm of this picture and your part is to keep in harmony with his ideas. Even when you are SITTING you can regard this as something which your character has chosen to *do.*

Your character, Julia, you'll discover, has thoughts and emotions which belong to her alone. Her emotions bring about any gesture she makes.

FACIAL EXPRESSION is also GESTURE which comes from the thoughts and emotions Julia is experiencing.

The secret of gesture lies in THINKING and FEELING as the character; in real life a gesture comes *just before* speech - and so it must be on stage.

To take a simple example: suppose Julia is horrified at something just said to her. This will show on her face *just before* she speaks. Don't ever *pretend* a look of horror for her. Believe and feel that you, as Julia, are truly dismayed and your face will register the emotion. Gestures made with the body follow the same 'rule'.

"Look!" says Props, "There's your cake stand", and she points to the table. If you watch carefully, you'll notice that her finger points at the stand a split second before she says, "Look!"

Remember: it is Julia who chooses a gesture. *Your* everyday gestures won't do at all, nor will artificial responses made without inner feeling.

Gesture and movement from Julia must take account of her age, personality and the times in which she lives. Think, for example, of Mary the Victorian servant. She didn't nod her head to her employer as if to say O.K. and flounce off to do her bidding. She bobbed a respectful curtsey as she said, "Yes Ma'am" and sedately left the room. How interesting it'll be to play Julia; a 20th century modern girl, I can't see her curtseying etc..

A final point: Gesture and movement are best thought out and selected or discarded when you are on the move and working with other players at rehearsal. *Then* practise at home.

NARRATOR'S NOTES:

Although we're skating over the subject, talking about gesture gives Bee an inkling of how to see her character WHOLE. When she knows her lines, she'll start being Julia. Meanwhile we continue with tiny bits of the jigsaw that she can eventually fit together herself...

Timing - in character:

Dear Bee,

So! You've been reading through the play. Always a satisfying thing to do.

Trust you to pick out the worrying bits first. It won't be as hard as you think to waltz on stage with a partner. That's what rehearsals are for. Still, here we come back to MOVEMENT and it is as Julia you will dance.

I remember one play in which a player had to dance a tango while keeping lines going. Fortunately, like you, she shared the difficulty with a partner who led her around the stage.

As the director found it impossible to help while they flitted hither and thither he left it to them to work out timing the lines with movement.

Because the lines had to make the audience laugh, they practised swinging so that the person speaking faced the audience. After hours of rehearsal they finally got it right. Over and over they had played the tune on a tape recorder working out where the rhythm would allow them to stop in one of the poses of the tango.

They had, of course, to keep in mind *who* they were. Gradually, the characters - sophisticated 'artificial' people - *their* rhythm and that of the tango all became one in the players' minds. In this way, movement and the timing of lines dovetailed so that in performance, a young couple of high society danced in a (seemingly) effortless way while carrying on a witty conversation.

When you come to play 'Julia', you won't regret the time and labour you'll spend on the waltz. To work in harmony with a stage partner is one of the greatest pleasures in acting.

Think about it Bee: without attending to MOVEMENT and TIMING in CHARACTER a scene like this would fail.

It won't.

Costume - and set:

Dear Bee,

Glad you like the part. Having said that, isn't it a bit soon to start gathering together the clothes you'd like for costume?

Let's say that it's never too early to start visualizing your character along with the kind of frocks you might wear; a romantic fluttery idealistic teenager, the clothes Julia chooses will fit the image she has of herself.

At the same time, although thinking about style adds to your understanding of her, keep in mind that the final word belongs to the director, who can seldom grant a player individual choice in either costume or colour.

Why? Imagine a set painted in delicate blues and greens. Further imagine that both the leading lady and you, her stage daughter, without consulting each other decide on wearing pale blue and green.

In the first place, for both players to appear in identical colours presents a dull picture for the audience. In the second place, neither of you would stand out against the scenery. (A case of 'The Disappearing Cast'.)

With men it is not as difficult, though Wardrobe must check that three men will not appear, say, in fawn tweed jackets and brown pullovers, whether or not they fade into the scenery.

Wait, Bee. Wait till you know the colour of the set with all its furnishings; wait till the director accepts your reading of Julia's character. Finally, wait for the evening when he discusses costume.

In a modern play produced by amateurs, the cast largely provide the costumes. You'll find that the women will exchange frank views on what and what not to wear.

Gradually a picture emerges made up of colours and textures which will eventually blend and contrast as players move about the set; a picture approved by the director. Only at this stage may you begin to make, borrow and find the frocks which will enhance, not you, but Julia.

Remember, that though no-one rehearses in performance costume, you can improvise by wearing clothes similar to them in length. This time you may get away with your mini skirt!

Men and women players should keep in mind, that if they are to put on outdoor clothes on stage they should practise this. Struggling into the wrong sleeve leads to struggles with lines - and just imagine the effect on the audience!

NARRATOR'S NOTES:

'Books down'

Three weeks later with rehearsals well under way and Bee trying to do without her script. This is a difficult time for the cast and director as they're all apt to get into the doldrums because of faulty lines and reliance on the hard-worked prompter.

Bee cheered up, however, to tell me that the director has decided on set and contrasting costume colours. The women have been getting into little huddles to discuss the absorbing subject of "what to wear".

Costume - 'which belongs':

Dear Bee,

Right! Stage appearance is "terribly important" - not so long ago you told me that the "soul is what matters."

Of course you're correct about both things, and we do agree (?) that costume is only important in so far as it forms the shell reflecting the personality within.

Your task now is to wear Julia's costumes as if she had been born in them; at times exaggeration is allowed! From now on, Bee, the time you spend on detail and fit and trying-on and discarding and selecting and discussing and despairing and hoping, is vital, for only *then* can you follow the players' unwritten rule: 'forget 'em'.

Our club hired most period costumes; these couldn't be tried on till the Sunday before dress rehearsal because funds didn't allow our having them for a longer period. This meant little practice in forgetting them. Your own club experienced this with your 'Mary' play.

NARRATOR'S NOTES:

I recall 'Dressing-up Sunday' as a day of desperate activity all mixed up with giggles and moans, when costumes were removed from their boxes and on to hangers. These scarcely had time to adorn the room before the arrival of the cast who whisked them off the wires within seconds.

Exclaiming over the goodies, players vanished behind screens to try them on. The others waiting their turn, could hear oohs and aahs and oh no-ings, shrieks of joy, muffled swearing from the men and their occasional explosive "No way! I can't wear that!" The cooing of the wardrobe team with their "Come on now, it only needs letting out..." punctuated these tantalising sounds as they coaxed the players into tight sleeves - and submission. Shows of temperament undreamed of, the cast got down to the business of making the costume 'their own'.

(Some time later: When Bee, along with the cast, met in the club room to try out their costumes, the director turned up to give his views!)

The 'right' costume:

Dear Bee,

It seems to have been an exciting occasion!

You must feel relieved that the director approved of your choice of costumes although I was intrigued by your remarks on a show of rebellion from one of the cast.

It seems that Mrs. Manners (interesting that she's playing your stage mother this time) refused to wear a frock she condemned as dowdy and the director considered just the thing. On thinking over even the little I know about her personality, she may have good reason to say it just won't *do*!

Players, as I've said, must agree in the end to what the director decrees - still - if she feels strongly that the costume is wrong for her character, she may say so. Directors are not dictators and I'm sure a compromise can be reached.

NARRATOR'S NOTES:

Bee has written to say that she wants to hear about the time her mother played in 'A Midsummer Night's Dream'.

Dear Bee,

You are talking about the only occasion on which our club aspired to Shakespeare and I suppose your mother told you of her 'tantrums' as Titania!

To start with, the costume filled her with absolute horror. She'd expected a flowing chiffon gown. Certainly chiffon, beautifully fashioned and of an enchanting shade, the minute costume (a mini skirt would have looked long in comparison) could not by any stretch of the imagination - or material - be said to flow.

In spite of her despair she behaved, I thought, with dignity. I mean she didn't scream; she didn't shout. Instead, placing the costume in front of the director, she uttered the incredible words: "I won't wear it. If I never go on stage again, I won't wear *that.*" And I think she meant it.

Looking back, this was a rare event for the club, when discipline flew out of the windows and in swept anarchy; Titania wasn't alone in her reaction to a costume.

As a cast, already un-nerved by blank verse, they found the unfamiliar costumes hindered rather than helped with how they'd imagined themselves in Elizabethan dress. The two heroines had a trying time with stiff brocade skirts and the men felt strange in short tunics and tights.

Jane and I both recall the bleak eye with which Hippolyta regarded the leopard skin assigned to her as Queen of the Amazons. (She had rehearsed as if in some kind of Greek robe.) That she agreed to wear it at all, says much for her fortitude. By coaxing someone into plastering her with sun tan dye every night (she spent hours in the bath that week) and arranging her dark hair on top of her head, in the end she looked beautiful but sad.

That they all survived - Titania received an exquisite chiffon skirt (long) by the way - remains a happy thought.

There's something to be learned from all this. Had the players been given time in which to 'forget' their outfits, a more joyous rendering of the play might have emerged. Players find it hard to come to terms with costumes which are not part of how they see the characters. All this certainly leads to some interesting permutations i.e. costume and character; character and movement; costume and movement... whatever, they bring with them sincerity of emotion when in harmony.

VI

COMEDY

Laughter:

(Bee is now into an exciting part of rehearsals):

Dear Bee,

-Mark in the laughs as you go- did you ask the director to explain those cryptic words? If not - do - it's always wise to ask the boss to explain!

To begin with: the play you're in is a COMEDY. Not all comedies set out to make the audiences roar with laughter, but the one you're in is very light and frothy and *does* require the audience to respond with laughter.

THE PLAYWRIGHT, the first person responsible for this effect, achieves this through a selection of humorous situations and the lines given to characters.

THE DIRECTOR's goal is to carry out these wishes. At rehearsals he will make more and more clear how he hopes to bring this about.

Finally: THE CAST - at this stage in rehearsal all the director wants from you is that you appreciate what is to come. To help you do this: Mark in the laughs i.e. put a cross at the places where the audience *must* laugh. The director will point them out to you.

Use of eyes

Dear Bee,

Have thought of another comedy 'point' for you to consider: the importance of 'eyes' in acting. An audience must see your eyes most of the time, otherwise they may as well look at a mask. Far too many amateur actors either look *through* their partners with glassy (unseeing) eyes, or they study the floor (at least their eyes are downcast) and when they do look up, still fail to make eye contact with the actors on stage. As far as these others are concerned, it's like speaking to a piece of wood or, if by accident their eyes do happen to meet, it's unnerving to look into a pair of frightened orbs which don't belong to the character s/he is supposed to be.

It's an odd fact that when players come off stage and say in puzzled (and hurt) tones, "I didn't get the laugh I got last night on..." such and such a line, they never realize it's because the audience couldn't see their eyes. In comedy you have to signal that a funny line is coming and it is the eyes which do the work a split second before you say the line. An audience likes to be in the picture: to see and hear the joke.

The acting point is, of course, that as the character, you must, before your laugh line, react for a scrinch of a second to what your partner has just said. Your face registers this feeling through the eyes - both of them! - and the audience are in the joke. Although they don't know what you'll say, they are in the mood to laugh.

NARRATOR'S NOTES:

...and thank heavens Bee has a rich sense of humour for this is valuable indeed when it comes to spotting where the laughs are.

The art of comedy playing, and indeed it is an art, lies in knowing *when* to make an audience laugh and *how* to do it. Bee will come to all this gradually, relying as much on her own powers as on the director's. Another team!

Overdoing the 'action':

Dear Bee,

That the director ticked-off your stage partner - what did he say? - something like "stick to suitable actions and what's in the script" - was probably because Simon annoyed him by trying to get a laugh where none was intended. Not that the director would object if what the boy was doing, added to the fun. Obviously it didn't!

Take note: inexperienced players sometimes become desperate either to please the director at rehearsal or eventually an unfortunate audience, in their efforts to 'get a laugh'.

I once saw this happen to an unhappy player who just couldn't make the audience laugh when they were supposed to. This young man splashed overboard in the middle of a one-act comedy.

In the scene, the character lifted a bucket and tipped the imaginary contents into the wings. With the bucket held high, not only did the player mime throwing the water but for good measure added sound effects: -whoosh, whoosh, whoosh, plop!- he gushed.

He got a laugh all right. How unfortunate that it was in the wrong place. Galvanized by the welcome sound of giggles, which he mistook for appreciation, the player strode to the fireplace where an old fashioned broom was placed. Grasping it, he attacked the floor. Merely flicking at the stage during rehearsal, he now swept with great rasping sweeps, bending to the task with the strength of an Atlas.

From the audience came a choked sneeze, then another and another, as the dust of ages swirled from the wooden floor and into the air. Flurrying in the stage lights, it descended silently, slowly, reverently on the bowed white head of the director. Alas! No longer white.

Atmosphere for comedy:

Dear Bee,

Saying lines in such a way as to make people laugh is a skill which to an extent can be learned and what can't be learned, you may well find you already possess.

The director, while trying to capture the moods and feelings contained in the written words depends on *you* to bring out the humour.

Let's concentrate on some of the ways you may enter into the spirit of the story by thinking firstly about ATMOSPHERE:

Suppose you arrive home to find an argument raging between members of your family. Your brothers are both present along with your mother and father.

You come in through the sitting room door dying to tell them about the amusing incident you witnessed on the bus:

JOHN: *(absolutely furious)* ...and don't try to get out of it -- you're always messing about with my things!

BILL: I never touched your miserable bike!

BEE: Hi everyone!

(No-one pays any attention apart from her mother who gives her a vague smile.)

JOHN: *(with heavy sarcasm)* Oh? And I suppose the force from outer space bent the wheel?

DAD: *(angrily)* Now listen to me! We're sick to death of you two arguing about...

BILL: I'm *not* arguing - I'm sick of him accusing...

BEE: I saw such a funny...

JOHN: Not as cheesed off as I am with your rotten...

MUM: Boys!

BEE: It really was hilarious...

BILL: Who's rotten!

And on and on it goes. With all these voices raised and tempers high, definitely *not* the time to tell your funny story. The ATMOSPHERE is *tense.*

Let's suppose further that in the middle of this uproar, your aunt and uncle drop in.

AUNT: We thought you might like to come for a drive - it's such a lovely...

JOHN: *(under his breath)* and don't think you've got away with it!

AUNT: *(bewildered)* What?

DAD: Stop it at once!

BILL: It's not me! It's John.

UNCLE: *(heartily)* Well? Are you game?

MUM: *(with an effort)* Yes, of course. We'd love to come.

JOHN: *(trying at last to calm down)* Yeah! Great!

AUNT: *(who's beginning to feel uncomfortable)* Right! Shall we go?

BILL: I'm not going if *he's...*

Of course it's hopeless. The family *(those who tried)* have not been successful in hiding their ill-temper. The visitors feel uncomfortable - THE ATMOSPHERE is *strained.*

If on the other hand the family are in high spirits when someone arrives with bad news - anyone who continues to laugh and joke will receive no encouragement - THE ATMOSPHERE is too *heavy* for trivial thought.

TAKE NOTE Bee: that when the overall ATMOSPHERE OF A COMEDY SCENE is not in harmony with the mood of the dialogue, it's just as impossible for an AUDIENCE to laugh and get into the spirit of a play.

Timing - use of pause:

Dear Bee,

We've thought about atmosphere in comedy, now let's look at TIMING and the use of PAUSE.

Here's a short play for you to think about. Believe me! It's not as far-fetched as it may seem. Scenes similar to this can take place.

Keep in mind that when a director is as inexperienced as his cast, the awful rehearsal outlined here would continue uninterrupted by any comments from him.

SCENE: *A club room in which a rehearsal is in progress. A young man on stage speaks his lines to another member of the cast. Abruptly he stops speaking and stands quite still.*

DIRECTOR: *(in wonderment)* What *are* you doing?

PLAYER: *(bewildered)* Nothing!

(a tiny pause)

DIRECTOR: I know that. *(pause)* I meant, what are you doing when you're not speaking?

PLAYER: *(a thoroughly blank pause)* I'm - well - I'm - it says here *(he refers to his script)* that there's a pause. So *(he stops and looks triumphantly at the director)* I'm pausing!

(a tiny silence)

DIRECTOR: I see. *(in controlled tones he adds)* What then are you *doing* in the - er - 'pause'?

PLAYER: *(patiently)* I'm counting.

DIRECTOR: *(taking a deep breath)* What did you say?

PLAYER: I'm *counting.* Look! *(he shows the director the place in the script)* Here! - in my first pause I only counted to 'three' before I spoke, because it says 'a short pause'. But in the one you stopped me in *(he casts a reproachful look at the director)* I was counting to 'six' because I felt it was a longer one!

(There follows a - dangerous? - silence.)

DIRECTOR: I see. *(pause)* And do you suppose that your character 'Tom' is counting when he pauses?

PLAYER: *(laughing kindly at the foolishness)* Of course not! He's just stopped speaking.

DIRECTOR: *(returning to his seat - he feels he must sit down)* Tell me - has it never struck you that 'Tom' might actually be THINKING?

Your first lesson in timing. A pause is for thinking in. (It's a bit more than that really.) How would you like to go over the play and let me have your thoughts?

NARRATOR'S NOTES - a few days later:

Was interested to have Bee's reactions. Sometimes it's better for either players or would-be players to worry out something for themselves i.e. when they know what they're looking for.

Dear Bee,

A good start! Yes, the overall mood of the director in the play is controlled annoyance: he pauses when he's thinking of the things he'd *like* to say, but doesn't! As you got that point, how about looking at the way his mood BUILDS?

Meantime - yes - the reasons for the young man's pauses vary from non-understanding, though that actually never changes, through reproach to a kind of smug explanation.

You're right when you say the pause for the director sitting down takes a lot of silent acting. In fact, of course, players silently act through any kind of pause given. N.B. Pauses only work if the player concerned makes the audience believe in the character.

Your other point that the playwright doesn't always use the word 'pause' is correct. He writes: -took a deep breath- or -looks reproachfully-. In *your* play you find: -Simon lifts an enquiring eyebrow- -Julia flung the book on the floor- -Her mother refrained from answering- -Julia turned away- and so on. All these are PAUSES for thought or action by the character.

By the way, did you notice the ATMOSPHERE of the scene? Would you agree that it allows gentle fun to be poked at the young man?

Your final point: "What did you mean when you said 'A PAUSE is a bit more than just thinking'?" Well, when you're getting to know Julia, study the pauses she's given. They're every bit as important as what she says. As she's a character in light comedy, often her pausing is a SIGNAL to the audience that what she's about to say will be funny. It makes them wait in SUSPENSE for her line.

Again, she may pause because she's unsure of what to say. Occasionally, she pauses because (for a change) she's not going to say the first thing that comes into her impulsive mind. Once or twice she pauses because she's stunned by something said to her... she pauses for a variety of reasons.

As Julia 'lives' throughout the play, the audience grow to understand her, sympathise with her and come to expect certain reactions from her. Sad when she's sad, happy when she is, often the playwright allows them to wonder what this surprising girl will say next. The audience will *share* Julia's pauses, as long as you, Bee, continue to make them believe in her. Technically, this doesn't mean that you necessarily pause for long: a pause may last the scrinch of a second, the time it takes to draw a breath.

When your line is one 'marked for laughs' your reward will be a burst of laughter from the audience which you'll have earned because of both pause and line (and of course because everyone is living along with Julia).

NARRATOR'S NOTES:

So far, so good! Bee and I have talked over important skills of comedy: atmosphere and timing of pauses. ...and when comedy timing becomes 'spot on', when Bee achieves the intentions of the playwright and director, she'll realize that the weeks of rehearsal have been worthwhile; and when the moment of performance arrives, she'll know the joy of filling a theatre with spontaneous laughter.

'Polish':

Dear Bee,

So happy for you that the people sitting on the side-lines at rehearsal are beginning to laugh at the right bits. As you say, there's nothing to beat the feeling you get when this happens.

Don't be frustrated that you can't give a polished performance. Apart from the fact that you've only just started, do you think that amateurs can hope for much more than a veneer of polish in a performance?

By that, I mean they don't have the benefit of a long run of a play in the provinces; they can't try out techniques on one audience after another; they miss out on the experience of coming to know a character over a long period of time and there's not the thrill of a London production.

NARRATOR'S NOTES:

...there's no doubt that the amateur's task is a hard one. With only two rehearsals followed by three or four nights in a theatre, when the curtain closes on the Saturday night so does the play. Sometimes on the Sunday, amateurs are left not only with the memory of excitement, but with a sense of anti-climax that lingers on into the weeks ahead.

Dear Bee,

That rehearsals continue to go well, is good news.

What a lovely thought you had about your 'lack of polish' worry. I agree with your summing up that being an amateur means that our 'haven't we done well' feeling is greater because of the odds. In other words: amateur players can prove that dedication, discipline and damned hard work bring their own reward.

We must talk later about the importance of partnerships on stage and in comedy particularly.

NARRATOR'S NOTES:

...though I'd like Bee herself to see the point that comedy moments are always shared. Meantime I know she'll be putting together the points already spelled out: atmosphere; timing; use of pause; laughter - and 'being in character'.

Essence of comedy:

Dear Bee,

So Simon's been yattering on about the heart of comedy (!) and you'd like to - er - know what he's talking about? That's a hard one, for there's so many aspects. Let's stick to a few 'essences'.

CONTRAST: essential to good comedy.

ACTION: without action, you wouldn't have any drama, let alone comedy.

PLOT: you'll find action at the heart of the story-line (or plot) in comedy and all drama.

AUDIENCE: who become interested in the plot when characters - their actions, appearance, situation and dialogue are full of CONTRAST.

NARRATOR'S NOTES:

I wonder if it's clear to Bee that whenever I tell her something, I take it for granted she always refers back to the play she's in - as well as to Simon!

Contrast in comedy:

Dear Bee,

With the play in front of you, read it again - and pick out points of CONTRAST.

Thinking about Julia, notice the variety in DIALOGUE:

In some of your scenes it flows gently.

In others the pace is fast.

Notice how the playwright *varies* the tempo:

Two scenes never follow each other at the same speed/pace. How is this done?

How many people are in a scene? (There is, for example, one scene with Julia and Simon which leads into a scene between Simon, Julia and her mother. The final scene of the act includes your stage father.)

Does the playwright vary the length of lines in each scene? (In the scene where you and Simon quarrel, for example, it builds to quite a storm, doesn't it?)

How about when your mother enters? (She, as a sophisticated and theatrical character sweeps you both aside, talking at a fast pace, while you and Simon slow down.)

When Julia's father enters there's another change of tempo. (He has his own quiet pace, mother has hers, and interestingly, Simon and Julia begin to perk up again. All this *variety* allows the act to end on a suspenseful note.)

Look again at the BUILD-UP to the climax of a scene in which comedy and action are the keynotes. (How well the characters contrast: in personality, in pace, in volume, in tone...)

You'll find VARIETY in every comedy you either read, or watch in theatre, for it's the *spice* of comedy!

VII

TECHNIQUE

Dialogue:

Broken lines:

Dear Bee,

You'd have more reason to complain about Simon *not* interrupting you on the lines you speak of!

In light comedy, BROKEN LINES - or - CUT LINES often turn up. This means that your partner *must interrupt* you on those lines.

One reason for them is to QUICKEN THE PACE. Aren't you and Simon quarrelling in that particular scene? As in real life, characters, when angry, break in on each other's words: as they can't wait for the other to finish speaking, you and Simon have to give the impression that you're not listening to what each other is yelling.

All the same, I expect what's troubling you is that Simon is overdoing it. He must let you get the important words out - *and* - he mustn't interrupt you on lines not marked in by the playwright for cutting. (It's known as OVER-CUEING.) Don't blame him too much at this stage: he's as inexperienced and enthusiastic as you are.

The answer lies in your both understanding the technique of handling cut lines. Interrupting someone happens all the time in real life; on stage you have to work on it to get it right.

Angry people, we've discussed. Incidentally, remember that imaginary scene with your family? - a lot of cut lines there! Excited people cut in: they can't wait to tell some news and break in on each other in their eagerness to be 'first to tell'.

And you've met people who won't let you tell a funny story on your own: they're dying to give the punch line themselves (exasperating habit!)

How often too, you've met those superior folk who imagine other people are so slow-witted that they must supply the words which you might have said - given the chance.

Look at the way cut lines are set out in a script e.g.:

JILL: I was walking down the hill when...

JACK: *(breaking in)* You saw me drop the bucket!

The trick is for Jack to come in with -You saw- as if his and Jill's line were one speech i.e.

-I was walking down the hill/when you saw me drop the bucket!-

Many a Jack finds this difficult. Why? Because he takes a breath to speak *after*

Jill's word -when-; this leaves a rather nasty gap of time and Jill with her mouth open, wondering what to say.

Jack must take a breath *before* the word -when- i.e. while Jill is saying, -down the hill-. Magic! This lets him come in ON CUE.

Another way is for Jill to help. This might be when she is faced with an awkward line ending in -and-,

JILL: You fell down and...

JACK: *(breaking in)* then you came tumbling after.

If Jill takes a tiny breath just before she says -and- i.e. -You fell down (breathe) and-

this gives our hero Jack time to breathe *with* her and triumphantly come in on time.

You and Simon should sit together in a quiet moment and agree on just when and where you're both going to breathe! In other words: rehearse the TIMING.

NARRATOR'S NOTES:

Bee doesn't know it yet, but it's fun working out the techniques of cutting lines. The important thing is not to OVERCUE i.e. players, if they get over-confident, can come in too soon and important words are lost.

Cueing:

Dear Bee,

CUEING? A cue is really a hint or a signal to your partner that it's his or her turn to speak. In other words, *you've* finished.

Don't get into the (bad) habit of listening only to your partner's last two or three words. Very dangerous: suppose he forgets to say them?

Look at the different ways you can take a word cue: When the pace is crisp, the actors speak as though there were no pause between the speeches. This is where your taking a breath *before* he's finished comes in useful. It's called QUICK CUEING.

Remember Mary? You stood outside the door 'waiting for your cue'. On such an entrance, it was no use hanging about till Mrs. Manners finished speaking, for by the time you'd got yourself and the cakes through the door, you'd have been LATE ON CUE.

What you had to do was work out the TIMING so that you could appear ON CUE.

As well, a cue is often needed for an effect off stage. In your own play Julia says: -It's not like him to be late.- This gives the stage manager the cue for the door bell to ring. It's important neither to forget the line nor to get it wrong.

'Getting it wrong' can cause things like this to happen:

ACTOR: Bert should be here soon. He said the signal's two rings on the bell.

(Panic backstage): the line should be: -He said the signal's two knocks on the door.-

Stage crew depend on you to say what you're supposed to say; on the other hand *you* depend just as much on them to respond to correct cues.

I remember an occasion when a player turned slowly to the fireplace and said: -We've let the fire go out.- (On cue, artificial flames leapt up the chimney.)

Get it right.

NARRATOR'S NOTES:

Words in context:

Bee doesn't like the word 'context'. Said it made her think of English exams. (Woe is me - and all that lark!)

Dear Bee,

As I tried to point out to you last night, it's not easy to tell you how to make sense of certain lines "unless I look at the context"(!)

Does this sound any better: I can't help you with meaning till I know what comes before your lines and/or what comes after?

In other words the context fixes the true meaning. Look at this: -I'll give you that- says Julia to Simon. Now what does she mean by 'give'? Does she mean that she's going to make him a present of something? Or does she mean that she'll agree with what Simon has just said? It depends on the CONTEXT, which you, as Julia, understand.

When you're struggling with the meaning of a passage and wondering which are the important words, try 'looking for the action'. Look for action in the verbs, as we did with the word 'give' that Julia used.

You don't need to hammer at the word: Julia didn't say -I'll *give* you that-

Hammering, or stressing if you prefer, depends again on the - er - context.

Examine the verbs in the passage worrying you. Ask questions of them: why has the writer used this verb instead of another? Does the final choice either change the meaning, or add to, or colour the thought differently?

-Don't say that- says Simon. Depending on the context, he could mean: -I'm shocked by what you've just said- or, -Heavens! If you mean what you say, we're in a fix!-

-He sounds a fool!- The exclamation mark in the script shows the player that the remark is an insult.

-He sounds a fool- (minus !) might mean that the character is not too sure.

Context gives you all the clues and it's up to the player to colour words in such a way as to make the meaning clear.

As well:

Make sure you're emphasising the KEY words.

EMPHASIS:

Placing the emphasis on different words can change the meaning of what's being said:

e.g. "I can do that"
Stress the word "I" - and you mean "You can but others can't."
Stress "can" - and you mean "please don't doubt me."
Stress "do" - and you mean "this is a choice I've made."
Stress "that" - and you mean "I can do that but perhaps not anything else."

Most importantly, you must understand the THOUGHT behind the words of your partner. (Please Bee *don't* learn your own lines without paying attention to another's.)

I said before it's of little use to learn only the last two or three words of your partner's lines i.e. your cue. (I called it a dangerous habit.) No wonder so many prompts hiss from the prompter's corner: if your partner ends up either with the wrong two words and/or changes the emphasis, you go blank. Why? because you haven't been listening to the SENSE of what's been said.

Apart from that, when you close your ears to THE MANNER in which your partner answers, you can't EMPHASISE and COLOUR your own speeches in correct context; the illusion of natural conversation fades into the wings, while the audience yawns its head off.

Interpreting dialogue:

NARRATOR'S NOTES:

Bee and Simon worked together on the scene and felt better about it. The director said they were on the right lines!

However gloom, gloom! He wasn't impressed by Julia's big scene with her mother - our Mrs. Manners. He didn't think their interpretation was clear. Bee wants to know *exactly* what he meant.

I wonder whether it's just Bee that's off the rails or are she and Mrs. M. both busy doing their own thing?

Dear Bee,

Look back at the notes I gave you on EMPHASIS. Are you absolutely sure that you're listening to Mrs. M. and replying to the sense of what she's saying? And/or is she doing the same for you?

The director has set the atmosphere - is the way in which you say your lines in keeping with this? Are both you and Mrs. M. working in harmony? (Read over the notes I gave you on LAUGHTER.)

NARRATOR'S NOTES:

Bee says she had a worthwhile discussion with Mrs. M. She told her she was worried by what the director had said and asked whether she felt Julia was on the wrong rails.

Mrs. M. suggested that they both work on the scene together and stretch the threads of meaning tight between them. This is not only kindness but for my money, shows why she is a lead player.

Dear Bee,

Glad you had the talk with your stage mother; she's so right about 'meaning' - without it neither of you would be able to communicate the characters' thoughts to the audience!

You say you're fascinated by the idea of colouring words. Let's look at that more closely:

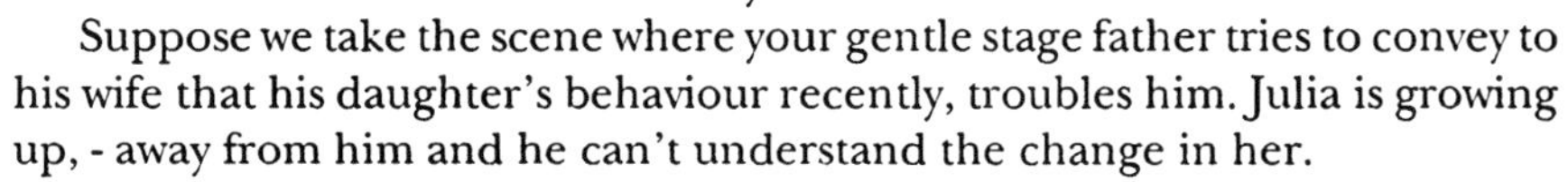

Suppose we take the scene where your gentle stage father tries to convey to his wife that his daughter's behaviour recently, troubles him. Julia is growing up, - away from him and he can't understand the change in her.

In his mind perhaps he rejects the following:

-I am appalled by Julia's behaviour-

-I am disturbed by Julia's behaviour-

-I am worried to death by Julia's behaviour-

Every one of these verbs contains what he means, but as it's not in his nature to give voice to such words, he says instead, -I must admit that I'm *uneasy* about Julia's behaviour-

Somehow Julia's father must convey to the audience that his true meaning is behind the word he chooses. To put it another way, the actor must COLOUR the word with unspoken thoughts.

Are you giving enough weight to unspoken thought? Look at the following example. Perhaps it'll help you understand shades of meaning in the voice when the words appear to say something different.

-Do you like my new frock?- Julia asks Simon.

-Yes. I think it's great.-

Now this answer can be said quite sincerely; the words mean exactly what they say.

But suppose Simon feels the frock is ghastly; the way he says -it's great- doesn't quite hide his true feelings; and if he's in a bad mood he'll hope you get the message. As you can see, Simon, learning this line, has much more to do than memorise -Yes. I think it's great.- Try saying these lines with their different meanings.

Words often cloak meaning i.e. give out opposite messages from their true meanings. In a well-written play you have to search for the subtle and contrary meanings hidden in the context.

Finally, let's concentrate on how the EMOTION changes when words are coloured differently. Let's use one sentence and see what happens when it's spoken in different contexts:

-He said he would come *to-night*- (not to-morrow).

-He *said* he would come tonight- (tonight's the night).

-He said he would come tonight- (anguish at the thought that he may not come now).

-He said he would come tonight- (don't argue; I'm telling you he comes tonight).

-He said he would come tonight!- (dismay at the thought of him appearing tonight).

Shade - tone - context - stress - emphasis - pause - emotion - character... plenty to think about!

NARRATOR'S NOTES:

For the last week or two, rehearsals have been going well and Bee has been in the seventh heaven about the play, the cast, the director and her part.

Unfortunately, there's always a point in rehearsals when things don't exactly go wrong but the director starts to insist on everything being right; Bee finds she's doing things that don't please him which she'd never even thought about.

Posture:

Dear Bee,

All right, the director seems to be gunning for you. Feel encouraged; he thinks you're worth worrying about.

What if he does criticise your carriage (a quaint word, you scoff). He obviously feels that the way you hold yourself is not in keeping with Julia's character. Long ago we discussed the importance of walking in character.

On the other hand your director is also referring to the posture and elegance of the trained actor: with head straight, shoulders down, arms relaxed, legs moving from the hips - not the knees - what a joy to watch an actor move in this way.

Being on stage is like being under a microscope - anyhow, everything you do is done under the eagle eye of the audience, so carriage, posture and movement must all be spot on. Funny thing, but even when an actor takes on the role of someone bent and slouching, if he or she starts off as a perfect 'specimen' this allows them to act with an inner authority.

NARRATOR'S NOTES:

Watching Bee play 'Mary', I thought her bearing on stage was good; wonder if the director's getting at something to do with the CHARACTER of Julia?

Dear Bee,

FEET? You do set some problems! I don't know whether the director is referring to the way you move *your* feet or whether he's talking about Julia's feet. (I realize that he's a little harassed at the moment and flits away before you've got a full answer.)

Let's suppose he's talking about *your* feet:

Before you move off in any direction, make sure that your feet know what you're about to do e.g. balance the weight on the left leg when preparing to move RIGHT and vice-versa when moving LEFT. Very important not to let your legs get tangled up.

If, on the other hand he's talking about character, then let me tell you this tale:

A friend once gave me a pair of 'pointy' shoes which she thought might be useful in a play. However, as they were a bit tight, I put them in a cupboard.

Some years later I played the part of an elderly spinster who had seen better days. She wore a feathered hat squashed well down, my grandmother's tiny fur stole tight up to her neck, a shapeless coat, woollen stockings, and bag clutched in both hands. At rehearsal I was delighted with her. And yet, when I looked at her in the glass, I could see something was missing. At that point I remembered the old-fashioned shoes!

I tried them on. Drawing on shabby gloves, I clasped the bag, tightened my lips and feeling like Andersen's mermaid, for the pain was excruciating, teetered forward. She lived and breathed and MOVED.

What is Julia wearing on her FEET?

NARRATOR'S NOTES:

Seems to have been Julia's feet. Bee was wearing 'flatties' at rehearsal (she'd forgotten that what I said about 'Mary' wearing appropriate shoes, holds good for all plays). The director is delighted by her change of footwear; apparently she's got herself into what she terms a silly pair. Good!

Projection:

Dear Bee,

Two more complaints? You are having a bad time. Do keep in mind that clubroom rehearsals are coming to an end and everyone is a bit uptight.

Project? The director possibly thought you were mumbling and so, shouted the word at you from the back of the room. Think of it this way: if *he* can't hear you in rehearsal then *we* won't hear you in the theatre. It doesn't mean he's asking you to shout. The audience won't care for it. Just take thought for your granny in the back row who doesn't know your lines. At least that's how O.C.D. always phrased it. After a telling pause, he'd add, "She's paid as much for her seat as the woman in the front row."

Mumbling and muttering have to do with faulty voice production. In the meantime, practise deep breathing, relax, unclench your teeth so that sound can get out and think of your granny.

Projecting, however, is easier to think about if you concentrate on the idea of sharing; don't waste all the hours of rehearsal by not communicating your character's thoughts to the audience.

NARRATOR'S NOTES:

Bee's problems can be solved, eventually. Little use to say to amateurs, "Go and have lessons in voice production" for some can't understand the necessity, some can't spare the time and some don't have the cash for private lessons.

One idea is for club members to badger their committee into spending a little of the profits on either paying a 'Voice' teacher to give some lessons or, better still, joining up with other clubs. Expense is thus shared and the problem is on the way to being solved. Weekend workshops on voice production, acting and make-up are not only huge fun but you learn a lot.

Smiling:

Dear Bee,

Let's deal with the other complaint: the director thought you should smile more often... it's odd, but looking into my storehouse of visual memories I can't recall many players who smiled on stage. Oh, I'm not talking about the stretching of closed lips, not the twitching of facial muscles, not even the baring of teeth while the eyes remain blank. There's plenty of them around.

But what about the real heart-warming glow that softens the face, that reaches wide-open eyes which look at you as if pleased to see you; the smile that embraces an audience and takes them into the character's confidence?

It's worth a try.

NARRATOR'S NOTES:

Although I do remember one or two players, I never told people that they had a lovely smile, for somehow or another they never got it right the next time.

(Some things are best left undisturbed by comment.)

On opening my scrap-book I see a group of smiling actors (!) radiating warmth to an audience. Ah, but wait! The photograph was taken *after* a performance, and the cast are standing in line to take their curtain call.

VIII

MORE THAN TECHNIQUE

Finding the character:

Dear Bee,

There's a limit, I agree with you, as to how much technique can help you in playing Julia. Now that you're making use of, and improving upon, all we've discussed, it's time to find Julia in other ways.

From the kind of things you say, it's clear that you realize what makes her tick; you've developed good relationships with Simon and your stage mother and father. As well, because you've worked at it with them, you are aware of how they relate to your character.

May I suggest that you never forget this is light comedy? It's a very funny play with the atmosphere buoyant, carefree and generally, though there are black moments, happy - and it's within that atmosphere the characters live.

Because it's a well-written play the writer allows his players to develop. Not long ago, you remarked that at the end of the play Julia didn't seem to be such a twit. In other words, she's not quite the gauche young girl of the first act! Slowly she changes and matures throughout the play.

In that connection, remember that *you*, as Bee, know far more about Julia in the first act than the audience do. It's a good idea not to give away too much till the moment in the script arrives for you to start communicating your knowledge.

So far so good. You've worked hard on this part and used your intelligence to reach an understanding of her. But we both know that there is even more to Julia; and this is the Julia you must search for yourself. Like you, she is a young and happy girl, waiting for life's surprises with optimism; it's not too difficult to empathise with her.

All the same, Julia is not you. So where and how is she different? In other words, how much of yourself can you bring to the part, and how much must you search for her?

And where to look? Not all Julia's experiences have come your way, so perhaps if you can think of 'like' things which have happened to you, you may reach a true understanding of her. Somehow or another you must find yourself saying: If I *were* Julia, I'd do it this way.

Struggle on, for *how* you reach such sensitive feeling for Julia is up to you. From now on, in these final rehearsals, both cast and director will concentrate on character.

NARRATOR'S NOTES:

Wonder if Bee will use any questioning of Julia, the way she did with the part of Mary and whether or not she's given Julia a background she believes in? Perhaps, but on the other hand, she may already be looking for her own ways-in.

Ah well! Analysing and 'soul searching' require care. As Julia is a happy-go-lucky girl it won't do Bee any harm to wrestle with the whys and wherefores of her character.

Where on earth, though, does one call a halt? No matter that audiences say lightly, "So and so lived the part", it's just not true. Why, if one took that to a logical conclusion this would mean players committing murder - or getting married - on stage!

Analysis:

Dear Bee,

So! Sitting up till all hours of the night, struggling to analyse Julia turned out a disappointing exercise. Now you're wondering why, after all your efforts, Julia is further away from you than before.

First of all, Bee, don't run away with the idea that *what* you did, was wrong. All good players spend time and effort in creating the character from within; it's to your credit that you tackled it.

Having said that, may I suggest that you don't lose sleep over Julia? For one thing you won't be fit for everyday life the following morning, and for another, sometimes the best work is done during rehearsals while relating to other characters. You can follow that at home by studying the play while you still retain memories of the rehearsal. You will, eventually, work out your own ideas on this.

Meantime: *don't* become obsessed with analysing character. Instead, listen to and discuss with, your director, the various facets of Julia's personality. After all, she must fit in with the play as a whole and not wander off into areas not required either by the director or the author.

NARRATOR'S NOTES:

Discussions with director:

I expect Bee's director would dearly love to have time to discuss in depth, with each player, the motives and tangled webs of relationships within the play.

A good director tries to let fall pearls of wisdom, a few at a time at each rehearsal. Experienced players aware of this, listen, not only to advice on their own character, but on remarks aimed at others. I have no doubt that Bee will get there in time.

Obviously, if this were a serious drama, the director *would* find time for lengthier discussion; as long as players are discouraged from using these as an opportunity to wallow in emotion, these talks are valuable.

Note to Bee:
Dear Bee,

Glad you noted my remarks. Further, while your idea of speaking to the director about your worries is fine, do find a suitable time to do it!

NARRATOR'S NOTES:

Bee's reply to my letter, which I think she wrote in a fit of the giggles, was a 'Dramatic Rendering of What Happened When I (tried) to Speak to the Director'.

TIME:	*Five minutes before rehearsal is set to begin:*
STAGE MANAGER:	Right! Everyone ready - cast for Act 1 please!
MRS. MANNERS:	We'll have to hang on. Simon's nipped out for sweets.
STAGE MANAGER:	*(didn't catch his reply!)*

(Simon rushes in and hands out to different people the sweets they'd asked him to get for them.)

DIRECTOR:	*(to S.M.)* Well? Are we ready?
STAGE MANAGER:	Yep! Beginners please!
PROPS:	*(to Director)* I must have a word with you about the typewriter used in this scene.
DIRECTOR:	Later! Later!
MRS. M:	*(to Director)* Do you want me to wear the cloak in this scene? I feel I should wear it as it's...
DIRECTOR:	Yes! Yes!
PROPS:	*(irritated)* She can't have it *now.* It's being altered.
BEE:	*(to Director)* Could I just ask if this is where you want...
DIRECTOR:	For heaven's sake! Can we begin!

NARRATOR'S NOTES:

!!!!! Obviously everyone's getting excited - including the director!

Oh how players complain about shortage of time. Looking at Bee's scene you can see how many valuable minutes they themselves lost in chatter and the never-ending getting ready to begin.

The answer lies in discipline; it's up to the individual director to provide it by allotting time to the different groups requiring advice. In other words - it's all his fault?

Improvisation:

Dear Bee,

Your note arrived telling me that, wonders upon wonders, the cast are to have several improvisation sessions during rehearsals! You're lucky to have a director capable of taking (and interested in) improvisation. Believe me, this will let you breathe a while and you'll enjoy the experience.

"What is improvisation?"

"I'm the Pirate chief, you're the bosun - and - and - oh you're the deck hand. Now (with a broad and magnificent sweep of the arm) here's the ship - and just here (pointing) is the bridge where I stand. Bosun, lock up the prisoners. And you - scrub the deck. Hand me yon telescope - a merchant ship approaches. All hands on deck! Man the guns!..."

Remind you of anything? I remember! I remember that as a child you and your brothers took part in such improvised (making it up as you go along) stories. Sometimes you were the bossy one in charge (though, more often than not it was John telling you and Bill how to scrub the decks). Age and weight counted!

Adults stayed out of the way. So - no-one to say, "Now Bee, don't turn your back on the audience." No-one to yell, "Speak Up!" for you played in an imagined world and your speech fitted the needs of the situation. No-one to moan, "Why do you stand like a stookie? Try to move naturally", for without the techniques of theatre to cope with, you moved with ease as you fought battles, Florence Nightingaled the wounded or flew through the air on a broom stick. In that lovely childhood world, you discovered everything was possible. No half-hearted phrases like "I'll pretend" ever entered your head; you *were* the witch. You said "I *am*" and "You *are.*" Who needed anyone to pretend?

Taking part in improvisation doesn't mean that you're divorced from your beloved acting: I'm always going on about being 'flexible': just imagine recapturing that child-like spirit when, free in body and mind, you concentrated your whole being on the essence of character. As you now realize, adults need to work to achieve this result in ways not known to a child.

Fortunately, actors can still learn from children by using improvisation as a way-in to character. They can experiment by improvising on scenes from the play. Use this (rare) opportunity to bring imaginative and deeper understanding to your interpretation of Julia.

If players changed the stubborn attitudes that some clubs hold whenever the idea of improvisation is put forward a new era in amateur acting might come into being.

To let you see what does happen when improvisation is suggested, I enclose the following. (I'll admit to exaggeration, but still...)

SCENE: *Committee meeting in club room.*
(You've met this committee before.)

SECRETARY: The director we've invited wants to take the cast through some improvisation at the beginning of each rehearsal.

DIRECTOR: Good Heavens! What next!

PRESIDENT: *(placating)* Perhaps we should hear what she says in her letter. *(She looks at the secretary.)*

SECRETARY: We-e-ll- she says *(she skims the letter in front of her)* 'Some of the cast are new to acting. They would benefit from the freedom of movement to be gained from using space as they please...'

COMMITTEE MEMBER: Some of the more experienced players could do with a bit of that!

(the president frowns at her)

SECRETARY: Shall I go on?

(the president nods)

SECRETARY: *(continues)* Mmm! - yes - 'in acting-out scenes in their own words, and in taking on different roles from the play.' *(She looks up.)* She then goes on about this helping them understand the other characters.

STAGE DIRECTOR: That'll be the day!

DIRECTOR: Silly woman! She's got no idea! Good heavens, it's difficult enough to get through even what has to be done, without wasting time on all this - this nonsense.

SECRETARY: *(ignoring him and continuing with letter)* 'and to those who would argue *(she smiles at director)* that there is not time for this type of work, just tell them that more can be done in a half hour improvisation than in two hours pushing players into stage positions...'

DIRECTOR: Cheek! She means me!

SECRETARY: *(cont.)* 'particularly when the end result is that beginners remain as stiff as before.'

DIRECTOR: *(grins reluctantly - the invited director is an old sparring partner)* Impudence! - she's accusing us of not knowing our jobs!

PRESIDENT: *(patiently)* No - she's only asking us to think again about some of our views on rehearsal. *(She braces herself.)* After all, it's true! Rehearsals - especially MOVES rehearsals - end with hardly anything achieved... *(the director leans forward in his seat)* - - -by some directors, because although they're O.K. with actors who know what they're doing, they just don't have the time to help beginners as much as they should - I mean, as much as is necessary.

STAGE DIRECTOR: *(puzzled)* But what's the point of them acting in a space, when in the end they've got to get back on the stage?

SECRETARY: *(her eyes searching the page)* Umm - ...'nothing but good comes from the cast working in a large space, using scenes from the play as a basis for improvisation.'

DIRECTOR: *(grunting)* Huh! As usual! She's got an answer for everything!

SECRETARY: *(cont.)* 'Apart from anything else, the cast come to rehearsal after a day's work with their minds full of everything but the play. Improvising allows them to unwind...

COMMITTEE MEMBER: Seems to me they all 'unwind' in chit-chat!

SECRETARY: Do let me get on! *(cont.)* Because no-one criticises them --- *(Dir. snorts)* --- ideas come to them which will help them with characterization. The mood in which players then begin rehearsal is as different as mealy pud. from pâté.'

DIRECTOR: *(heavily)* Very funny!

SECRETARY: *(laughing at him)* - - - 'and those players who sit around most of the evening waiting to be called, have enjoyed moving and acting - and doing something worthwhile for the play.'

(long pause)

SECRETARY: *(looking at the president)* Well? What have I to answer?

Bee - I'd love to end this scene with the committee's unanimous "Let's do it!" Alas, it's more likely that the meeting will drift on till eventually the committee will instruct the secretary to say (whatever way they word it) No!

Actually, the invited director would have been better advised not to write at all and prove the point with a successful production. If she has any sense that's what she'll do the next time.

To be fair, Bee, many clubs are already adventurous in their methods of rehearsing. Some others should be careful, for a deadly 'sameness' can creep into presentations. And 'sameness' tarnishes the brightness and colouring of directors' work and players' acting.

Besides, think of faithful audiences; a fresh approach which shows in 'zinging' performance stimulates them into encouraging others to "go and see this club's latest production - *everyone* in it is marvellous!"

IX

THEATRE

---

1) BEFORE GOING ON:

Timing - and stage furniture:

Dear Bee,

Theatre rehearsals time again!

You find 'real' furniture on stage, after the jumble of familiar old chairs and odd pieces used in the club room, definitely off-putting. It does take a bit of getting used to.

What can you do about it?

In the first place a chair is - for sitting on! Odd, that on stage, it seems to take on a life of its own. There stands this piece of wood, perhaps shaped into an armchair reclining downstage, or perhaps it's a dining-room chair standing to attention by the side of the table, or simply a humble stool crouching by the fireplace.

Whatever its size or shape it can present difficulties for beginners who, at some point in the play, require to walk to it - move round it - or even sit on it.

Suppose you are to sit on the chair by the table. At rehearsal you entered through the (imagined) door, crossed to the table and sat down with the chair already set for you at an angle.

On this, the First Night, a stage hand has pushed in the chair. You are unaware of this as you stand behind a (real) canvas door waiting for your cue to enter. Here it comes. On you go, cross to the table and prepare to sit. Woe is me etc.. You'll have to pull the chair out first. You lift it into the correct position and sit. Victory!

A silence follows: timing gone - you've forgotten your lines.

Let's try the armchair. The property mistress has, unknown to you, added several plumped up cushions. You sink back gracefully, but heavens! There you are perched like a hen on a dyke - bolt upright! Disconcerting.

Sofa? The angle at which it's set, doesn't allow you to face the other actor sitting on it with you, unless you turn a bleak profile to the audience. Not a position from which to speak your hilariously funny lines.

How are you to cope with any or all of these irritations? First: don't waste time blaming people. Take your troubles to the director who will pass them on to the stage manager, who will then deal sternly with the stage crew. Really the stage manager is largely to blame. Everything on stage must be checked before 'Curtain Up'. Second: realize the horrid truth that even in the best of clubs these things happen. What you do is: guard against as many calamities as possible. Get the stage manager's permission to wander around the stage and 'try out' all the furniture. When you're waiting to go on stage, take a peek and *check for yourself* that everything's where it should be. This gives you time to re-think should anything be wrong. Keep your wits about you and take *nothing* for granted.

Have a great dress rehearsal. I'm sending you a wee day-dream which may help you to visualize movement through a labyrinth of wood:

Sit in the auditorium and gaze at the stage, empty meantime, of people. Light floods the scene; it bathes the room, while cunningly placed stronger light ensures that centre stage is well lit, as are the armchair down right and the carved chair by the desk to the left of stage. And all this so that, when players have important lines to say, no shadow falls across them. Look well: the furnishings are destination points on the stage map as you move into different areas of the world you inhabit for a few hours.

In your mind's eye, you enter from the French window centre back and stand poised to speak. Below you, and to right and left, are the chairs which help your passage through the story. A movement across stage brings you to the stool where your mother sits. A neat turn and you are above and to the right of the sofa where Simon sprawls. Now you pause, turn, and move to perch on the end of the sofa. Soon, a quick cross to the desk where you sit to search for a letter.

Later, you rise, moving above centre stage to the tip of the rough triangle made by the positioning of the furniture - these guides - these allies. A cross to the French window where you turn again, your gaze taking in all on stage; finally a sweeping exit to applause from an ecstatic audience.

"On stage! Beginners, please," a bellow from back stage and in the darkened theatre you stir, wipe away the blissful smile of fantasy, and go back, refreshed, to the damned hard work of acting.

NARRATOR'S NOTES:

Tonight was the dress rehearsal. Kept thinking about Bee and hoping all was going well.

(Interrupted at this point by a telephone call from Bee. Thank goodness! Everything (mostly) went without a blessed hitch.)

One remark however, sticks in my mind; her casual reference to the furniture. She said, "I'm enjoying the 'real stuff' now. It helps to look natural when you can lean on the back of the sofa and things like that." The first bit's bad enough without delving into "things like that"!

On thinking it over, Bee has enough on her mind at the moment and I'll mention the awfulness of drooping over furniture at some other time.

Dear Bee,

My last note to you before the first night's performance and it's just to say that I wish you well and hope that everything goes as you would wish. Stick to what you've achieved in rehearsal and (as O.C.D. always said) enjoy yourself!

2) PERFORMANCE:

NARRATOR'S NOTES:

Nerves:

Decided to let Bee get the first night over before going to see the play.

Her family went, and according to Jane the performance was excellent: "Very funny and Bee did all right!" She added casually that she'd pop in and see it again on Saturday!!!

A late phone call from Bee who, after the show, had gone with some of the cast to Mrs. M.'s for coffee. Bee seemed in good spirits, dithering between excitement and relief that the first night passed without disaster. All the same, she admitted that she'd been so nervous her mouth dried up.

Poor Bee - 'nerves' are the very devil.

A note delivered to Bee the following day:

Dear Bee,

So glad you're happy about most things, though I'm sorry about the old nerves. Unfortunately they refer to well-known feelings suffered by those waiting to go on stage.

Taking a positive approach: remember that you're not the only one; it's possible to control 'nerves' and they generally disappear once you're on stage. The trouble about not being alone in your misery is that you've to fight against feeling that you don't give a hoot that your partner is jittery. You feel, if you feel at all, that if he'd only pull himself together, you yourself would be O.K.. As his thoughts are probably running on the same lines, you are, after all, sharing a feeling of self-pity.

I tell you, Bee: sometimes when I stood in the wings it felt as if I were on a desert island. It didn't matter that I could hear the voices of the lucky ones now safely onstage, for everyone in the theatre was part of a mirage; they didn't really exist. In any case I knew I'd never see home again, this moment would last forever and I'd be as old as Rip Van Winkle before my cue came. While the 'Curtain Up' music was playing, I waited for the tape to end and the only thought I ever thought was, "Why didn't I take up badminton?"

The point is Bee, that I lived through it all and learned to accept 'nerves'. So, if you can see yourself in anything I've said, then laugh with me.

You will, I promise, learn to control them; whether this is because your nerves decide they've had enough of you and simply can't go on in this way, or you do come to terms with them, I've never worked out. Perhaps what helps the most is that, through time, you'll become more aware of other people.

This awareness has something to do with close friendships (being part of the team) with the warm enveloping atmosphere of theatre, with the knowledge that an audience waits for you to do your best; something to do with all the rehearsals that have brought you to this point; something to do with your director...

Perhaps, above all, it's the determination that come hell or high water, you aren't about to fail either them or yourself. Dedication? Discipline? I never cared for badminton anyway. Did you?

NARRATOR'S NOTES:

Looking back, I can only marvel at the different ways different players coped with nerves.

In the end, I think those who coped best were those who either had the gift of retiring into a private world or had trained themselves to do so a few minutes before their entrances. It was as though other players went out of their minds as players. Soon we would all meet as people in the world of the play.

Bee's future experience will be largely with friends who will help her through the worst. And the worst will never be as bad as she thinks. Well, hardly ever.

Taking a prompt:

(In reply to a note from Bee after the second night.)

Dear Bee,

Everyone takes a prompt at some stage in their career so put the experience into perspective and learn from it. Your job now is to make sure it doesn't happen again tonight, at least not on these particular lines!

Have a word with the prompter to pin-point where you went wrong. You may have twisted a line just before the one you forgot, or been in the wrong position, or Simon may have given you a slightly muddled cue - or - ask yourself: "Do I know those lines really well?" Whatever, there is always a *reason* for absent-mindedness and once you've done all that's possible to avert another 'blank', forget the incident.

Did you feel aghast at my suggesting you may forget another line tonight? Don't be. Lines that vanish from your mind generally do so before you've settled in to the week's performances.

All the same, there's no harm in considering the possibility (not probability) that you may have another 'blank'; the trick is to take a prompt quickly then continue as though nothing had happened. A scene loses pace when the rhythm falters. Everyone must react to a prompt by crisping up the dialogue till the incident is passed.

Look over our discussion on the sense of dialogue. Think about the meaning of what *you* are saying, having listened to your *partner's* words. In this way, well-rehearsed lines should remain with you.

'Corpsing'

Dear Bee,

Corpsing? Who on earth introduced you to that word.

Meaning? - if you *must* know - it's an attack of giggles which you can't control, generally, and awfully, in the middle of a serious scene.

Cause? - *a lapse in concentration* which has led you to take refuge in something akin to throttled hysteria.

Consequences? - dire! For should the director witness you doing it - and s/he *will* - you're for the firing squad.

Advice? - Don't even *think* about it!!!

Good night!

NARRATOR'S NOTES:

...hypocritical - but probably safer - not to admit that actors, at some time or another, may give way to this - crime; perhaps not *all* actors, but on the other hand I've certainly met a few, like me, who have.

Sometimes it's brought on by people fooling about - the kind who respect neither their partners nor their audiences - these players the theatre can do without.

Involuntary giggling is different - its root cause is fear. The less Bee thinks about it, the less likely is she to give way to it - even if she has to swallow her tonsils; the effort would be preferable to giggling.

After the play:

Dear Bee,

Well done! The audience laughed from beginning to end.

I particularly enjoyed your big scene with your stage mother (a lovely mixture of pathos and laughter) and the scene with Simon where you have that hilarious argument! Your mother, though it's the second time she's seen it, laughed herself silly. So did I.

No doubt you'll feel a bit 'down' now it's all over, but console yourself with thinking how far you've come since your performance as Mary.

I shall tell you what I wouldn't tell you if it were untrue, that you have a future ahead of you as a player and a very good player at that. We must now wait to see what the future brings in the way of more experience in theatre.

There is now an interval of time - the summer lull - and so, if there are 'this and thats' you'd like to talk about just let me know.

POSTSCRIPT

Stage food:

Dear Bee,

You never mentioned eating on stage, and I'd forgotten that scene where Julia's munching an apple. No wonder you couldn't speak.

As for the others on stage and I quote from your letter: "...meanwhile Simon gnawed a chicken leg, waving it about as he wandered around the stage, and at dress rehearsal he choked. 'Mrs. M.' sat on the sofa nibbling a cucumber sandwich (it's when we get back from the ball) and Props piled a whole lot in to a sandwich and 'Mrs. M.' bolted off stage - she can't *bear* even the smell of cucumber let alone the taste. Rehearsing this scene was a Gloom!"

A gastronomic nightmare! The trouble is, that stage food must at least appear to be the real thing. Whatever way actors get around their indigestion, we, in the audience, want to see them tucking in to their 'vittles'.

It's like everything on stage: that the garden outside exists, that when you telephone, someone answers at the 'other end', that a real car drives up to a real front door... we believe in all these when - and only when - the effects convince us.

With fascination audiences watch while characters in play after play after play, chew and drink their way through soup, fish, meat, fruit, wine, coffee, tea...

However, tolerance and belief don't include accepting what is obviously 'pretend' food. Other effects may deceive, but there's a limit to John Bull and his friends' gullibility.

P.S. Julia would be better with a plum! As for Simon, he need only take small

bites while appearing to take large ones and 'Mrs. M.' requires nothing but butter on her thinly sliced brown fingers of bread. (We can't see that far.)

Remember though - actors must convince us that what's swallowed is - genuine grub!

NARRATOR'S NOTES:

Actors set limits:

Send Bee the following:

It's not only John Bull who has limits; for the actor there's also limits:

SCENE: a kitchen with the table set for breakfast. On the table: a packet of crisp cereal, a toast rack filled with toast, butter, marmalade, a boiled egg...

At the stove, mother is apparently poaching haddock. She carries a large tea pot to the table and pours tea into the cups.

Enter various members of the family who sit, pass plates, marmalade, butter, take cups, eat and *speak.* As, in reality, it's 8 p.m., the last thing the players want to do is face breakfast, far less swallow it.

Should this be opening night, appetite is even fainter, with tummy muscles writhed in knots, mouths like baked deserts and hands a-tremble among the cutlery. It may well be that in such circumstances thousands of amateur actors have enjoyed a good tuck-in; I just haven't viewed them across a table.

So! - to our moutons! 'A' shakes cereal into her dish, 'B' slices the top off her egg; 'C' butters a slice of toast, while 'D' gazes hopelessly at his plate of haddock.

And just how do they manage to convince long-sighted John Bull out there, that all is genuine and above board? With an imaginative Props, everything is possible: in 'A's dish is hot milk into which a few crunchy morsels descend and lo! a soggy mass results to which she now adds cold milk - spoon raised and down the throat it slips.

'B' meantime, pretends to slice an egg already cut by Props with the top cunningly replaced on an almost empty shell. Within may be a scrap of real egg mixed with a little butter - or - if 'B' has indicated that such a sight will induce her to make an unscheduled and fast 'Mrs. M.' like exit, then Props supplies chopped juicy orange or something as easily swallowed. 'C' is in a worse predicament with the 'seeable' toast. However, with only one side of the bread lightly toasted and spread with soft butter, he may manage to pop down a bite or two with the help of a cup of warm tea.

'D', (the one staring at his plate) has fish to cope with. Maybe 'D' doesn't care for fish and anyway has no wish to choke on a bone. And so, what he's faced with is food, but it's probably banana sliced lengthways and soaked in a sugary sauce. It slips down easily i.e. if 'D' likes bananas. If he doesn't? "Well," says Props, "you can dream up something for yourself!" Props too, has limits.

The trick is to make the food *look* what it's supposed to be - and - that it's easy to swallow. The only factor taking note of John Bull's prejudices is that the food is bona fide eatable stuff. Not even a great actor can eat papier mâché cereal and toast.

At rehearsals, however, if the actors have only pretended to eat, when food appears in performance which makes no allowance for dry mouths, horrid surprises await. Even when they've practised with real food, the outcome may still be disastrous; at rehearsals, throats are *not* dry, and the actors may eat with gusto.

Stage tea parties:

Dear Bee,

Yes, I do have painful memories of stage tea-parties, though they begin pleasantly with artificial sunlight streaming through the windows.

I recall the tinkling of spoons, the delicate nibble at cake... the sudden realisation that the dry sponge won't go down and "it's my turn to speak!"

With a shudder, I see the dainty cup and saucer poised in my left hand. My kind? hostess fills the cup to the brim. My right hand lifts it shakily and - there's simply no way that it can reach my mouth unless I bend over like a horse at a trough. So! I replace the cup on the saucer, whereupon the rattle and dithering of china falls upon the keen ears of Mr. and Mrs. John Bull. Believe me, Bee, ever afterwards I insist on the merest splash of warm coloured water in my cup and further, that when the cup descends to saucer, a scrap of tissue muffles the sound of its arrival.

Obviously, food isn't eaten in order to give the audience enjoyment; it's simply the enactment of a ritual familiar to everyone: stage business for the actor while he either listens or speaks.

There, literally, is the crunch; with a mouth full of dry biscuit, no words issue forth unspluttered; to wish someone "Good day" while choking to death is unacceptable.

And so, Bee, rehearse with minute pieces of moist food and practise when it is safe to swallow and when it is safe to speak i.e. TIMING bite, swallow, speech, listen, nibble, swallow, munch, drink, speak.

Keep in mind: food must never be too hot, too cold, too sticky, too dry, too much... there's always the interval when a brimming-over cup of coffee and rolls crammed to the gunnels with jaw breaking innards, await you.

Some clubs, striving for realism, go too far. A member of the audience remarked after a performance of a one-act play that her nostrils were filled with the smell of cheese wafting towards her from the plates of macaroni cheese on stage.

Easy to eat perhaps... this woman couldn't bear the smell of cheese...

And liquids too:

Liquids? Well! Audiences do accept that when players pour whisky or whatever, into glasses and drink heartily, they imbibe lemonade or cold tea. Paralytic performances are frowned on.

PART 2

ALL ABOUT DIRECTING

Apart from a brief look at the setting up of a drama club, this section is devoted to the business of being DIRECTOR.

Those of you who read the book for its survey of amateur acting, please don't feel that these chapters may be ignored. As the narrator so often reminds you, it's a good idea to look at problems from all angles - and there's no doubt that seeing things from a director's point of view is of value not only in coming to grips with characterization but in gaining closer understanding of relationships between players on stage.

The section is also intended as a painless method of recapping on various aspects of acting and in viewing some of these aspects at a deeper level.

For those who'd love to direct, my hope is that you'll find the following pages helpful and that some day, like Bee, you'll take on a production for your club. The amateur world is a little short on good directors.

X

BACKGROUND

NARRATOR'S NOTES:

As it turned out 'the summer lull' was not wasted, although Bee felt disappointed that she was not to be cast in next season's production. However, she is not given to long periods of despondency and common sense told her that one cannot, in a large club, expect to appear in every play.

She phoned to tell me that she is to help back stage. Mrs. M. is to be Property Mistress and Bee is to assist her. That Simon also volunteered for back stage work seems also to have - er - pleased her.

A break from on-stage work will be beneficial, providing the gap is not too long. There's a lot of living to be done and other activities to enjoy.

Mrs. M. and her husband enlivened proceedings by inviting Simon and Bee to come to Stratford with them in their car. They all put up in a hostel, attended several discussion groups on Shakespeare's plays, roamed around the bard's birthplace and paid several wonderful visits to the theatre. "Bliss!" said Bee.

On their return, Bee found a letter waiting for her. A group of young people who live in her home area had written to ask if she would be interested in helping them set up "a wee drama club".

An agitated phone call followed and I listened as she poured out all the reasons why she couldn't *possibly* take on such a task. "They want my *expert* advice," she ended, on a note wavering between laughter and disbelief.

"No," I managed a reply while she took time off to breathe, "you're not an expert but you know more than they do and they're obviously crying out for help. Perhaps you could explain that although your experience is somewhat limited, as long as they understood this, you'd be prepared to advise in any way you could?"

"Not on your life," said Bee, firm as the proverbial rock.

A few days passed before Bee wrote to me. She's recovered her wobbly self-confidence and said that she'd thought over what I'd said, and didn't say, and has told the youngsters she'll help. She added, "and as you're clearly set on my doing this, I wonder if you'd give me advice?" (!)

Dear Bee,

Don't think I can't appreciate why you turned down the youngsters' request at first. All the same, I'm glad you've decided to accept the challenge. More experience!

There's no doubt that it's quite an undertaking and you're wise to have pondered on the factors involved, before you begin. However, to encourage yourself, bear in mind that a group of young people asked for help and this shows there's need for such a club.

Setting-up a drama club

NARRATOR'S NOTES:

Before long Bee was on the phone to report progress. Five people are on the interim committee with Bee as chairperson.

The local tennis club reluctantly (said Bee) allowed them to use their committee room "for this time only" and the whole gang of fifteen turned up for an hour's hectic discussion on who should and who should not, be on the interim committee.

Bee said that when she arrived home, hot and confused, her father kindly handed her a little book on how to run a Meeting. Bee apparently glanced at it and her only comment was, "Ours was nothing like that!"

She has set up a first meeting with the new committee - meanwhile I'll send her a list of ideas she can start off with.

Dear Bee,

Glad you enjoyed yourself!

List of areas to think about:

A suitable hall in which to present plays.

Rehearsal space - at least a large room.

The use of a shed in which to make and paint scenery.

FINANCE: a pressing consideration!

NARRATOR'S NOTES:

I've given little advice in the meantime because Bee and the others will gain more by trying out ideas on their own.

Committee meetings

The day following Bee's first committee meeting:

Dear Bee,

Enjoyed your phone call! They certainly seem a lively bunch; it must have been hard work sifting out the workable inspirations from the - er - over the top ones.

As you say, you'll have to wait for them to report at the next meeting on how they've got on with "ferreting out possibilities."

NARRATOR'S NOTES:

On the phone Bee said that one of the boys in The Group (their interim name) has a married, older brother who is a member of a drama club in the neighbouring district. The boy, Andrew, is finding out if The Group could rent their hall for performances. Anne's Auntie possesses an enormous garden shed; Mark's Dad owns a hut on the waste ground below his working-garage, while James's Dad is a joiner... the only thing they never got round to discussing was money, or the lack of.

Bee's next meeting with The Group committee:

Dear Bee,

Thanks for letting me know what happened at the second meeting. I appreciate the dialogue you enclosed and that you've "left out most of the chit-chat and arguments we all wasted time on" is understood.

Bee's 'play':

CHARACTERS: Bee (Chairperson) (20+), Mark (18), James (17), Andrew (16+), Joan (18), Anne (18), Pat (17).

SCENE: *Bee's bedroom. Mark, James and Pat are sitting on the bed. Andrew is on the floor while Joan and Anne squash together on the blanket box. Bee has the only chair (to encourage a feeling of authority!)*

BEE: *(taking a deep breath)* Right! Stop talking everyone - try not to giggle, Joan - and let's find out what's happened since our last meeting.

MARK: *(a bit pompous)* Don't you think we should be a bit more formal...

ANNE: How?

MARK: *(vaguely)* Call the meeting to order and all that?

BEE: Consider it done - let's get on. Now *(she looks at Mark)* - you were to ask your Dad about the hut...

ANDREW: There's no use going on about the hut till we know whether or not we've somewhere to put the plays on...

PAT: Don't see it matters what order it's in. *(She looks at them over her specs.)* What I mean is we can't have one without the other anyhow.

BEE: *(hesitating)* Andrew has a point...

PAT: No he hasn't. He just wants to begin first with the hall!

BEE: *(a bit flummoxed)* Maybe Mark's right, after all. Perhaps we ought to have some order around here and after tonight we've got to research the correct way to hold a meeting!

(a pause)

BEE: Let's go on just now. Mark? *(She decides to begin with him after all.)*

MARK: Dad says yes.

(a pause)

JOAN: *(giggling)* Is that it?

MARK: Well - he wasn't keen at first but after I'd nagged on about it for a week, he said we could have the hut to store scenery and - er - paint in there - and so on.

ANDREW: Did he mention rent or anything?

MARK: No - he just said that if there's any hassle - or mess - or we broke anything - we'd be out on our ear!

ANNE: We'll just have to put someone in charge to see there isn't any mess.

MARK: *(grinning)* I think you'd better get on to it like yesterday. Dad sees it as a great chance to have his hut cleared out, so we've to crack on and do that first!

(They all laugh half-heartedly and Bee makes a note about Hut Clearing.)

BEE: Thanks, Mark. That's great. Now - Andrew! Any luck with your brother about us renting the Hall?

ANDREW: *(gloomily)* He said he'd have to think about it.

PAT: What's that mean? *Did* he think about it?

ANDREW: He said it wasn't up to him - he'd have to ask the committee...

PAT: And did he?

ANDREW: Did he what?

CHORUS: Ask the committee?

ANDREW: I expect so - they had a meeting last night and I'm to phone him for the answer.

(They all grab Andrew and push him to the door.)

BEE: The phone's downstairs. Get moving!

(A longish interval which they fill by cursing Andrew, with Pat dwelling on thumb screws. Andrew enters and flops down again on the floor.)

BEE: Well?

ANDREW: He says they want *you (he looks at Bee)* to attend a meeting to discuss it - and bring another member of the committee with you.

BEE: Right - who's going with me?

ANNE: Take Pat.

(All murmur agreement. Pat is pleased.)

JAMES: *(anxiously)* D'you think there's much hope?

ANDREW: Dunno. But they already let it out to other groups...

PAT: I bet they just want to suss out if we can pay the rent!

(silence falls)

BEE: *(bracingly)* O.K. What news about your Auntie's garden shed, Anne?

ANNE: Ouch! *(She's got cramp.)* She's more than not keen but I think it's yes. Anyhow, she wrote out an endless list of what she calls 'Musts' and we've to agree to the lot - or no dice!

MARK: Read 'em out!

ANNE: *(consulting list which Joan was sitting on)* We *must* be out of the place by ten o'clock - use the back garden gate - lock up after rehearsals - *only* use it for rehearsing - no parties - no smoking etc. - pay for heating and lighting...

MARK: Whew! Dad forgot about those!...

PAT: See you don't remind him!

ANNE: ...keep the place tidy - keep off the grass - keep the noise down - *and (her voice rises about the groans)* if we don't do *all* of that, we're...

MARK: *(grinning)* out on our ear!

BEE: Thanks Anne. *(She turns to James who never speaks unless it's strictly necessary.)* What did your Dad say about joinery, James?

JAMES: *(cheerfully)* He says he doesn't know a damn' thing about scenery but when we've found out how to do it let him in on the secret and he'll help. Oh - I forgot - he also said he's not forking out for wood - or anything!

BEE: I think you've all done well. *(She sighs.)* Next time we'll have to talk about *money!*

NARRATOR'S NOTES:

...penniless, of course, but a profitable meeting I think...

Matters arising:

Dear Bee,

Congratulations - you got through a power of business.

Perhaps when you meet the people-with-a-hall you should have some idea of the time when you will need it. As you've no money and no scenery as yet, you could set the first date some time ahead, though not too far away as this will be an incentive to get going.

Another idea is to make your first show a concert for which you won't require much scenery - in which case you won't need to wait so long to begin.

Think of it this way: a concert could bring in money. Dedication, discipline and damned hard work are required to *sell tickets!!!*

In the meantime I'm sure that committee of yours can dream up lots of ideas for making money - and for making other people toe the line.

During the coming months Bee, keep everything simple; at next year's first annual general meeting, the committee can present facts to be considered in the light of experience and the members air their views on what has and hasn't been achieved. That doesn't mean you can't have a meeting of the whole club fairly soon; you may find that many ideas worth listening to, come from the 'body of the kirk' and that should The Group decide on a concert you've lots of material.

Choosing a permanent committee:

I'm not sure when The Group will consider it necessary to form a committee elected by the club. Believe me when I say it's important for them to choose a committee carefully. You require a competent president to 'chair' the meetings and a hard-working secretary and treasurer. Where possible, the committee should consist of members who have, between them, a variety of interests. Just think of the agenda which comes up before a performance!

Appointment of director, (you may have to invite one) available monies, choice of play, notices to members, auditions, stage manager, theatre bookings, advertisement, posters, ticket sales, front of house staffing, meetings to be organised and so on and so on - an indigestible list.

To console you: when the positions of secretary, business manager and treasurer have been filled, your bread and butter affairs should run smoothly.

THE SECRETARY: a responsible position. Should you find one who takes notes which can be deciphered later, who can compose letters in a business-like way and who isn't afraid of making decisions, don't let that person escape. N.B. Whatever correspondence is sent out, the standard of writing reflects on the club - a courteous secretary is equal to the value of ticket sales!

TREASURER: a drama club is a business venture. What's the use of wallowing in highfalutin' ideas without a treasurer and committee capable of steering the club through the mundane and commercial side of life. No actors wish to play to empty houses. (Open a bank account.)

Appoint a chief director (you'll have one eventually). And there's no doubt that a stage director on committee is of value (in charge of Mark's Dad's Hut!) These two people can keep the committee's mind on the fact that the club is there for the purpose of *producing plays* of the highest standard possible. P.S. Do agree that you should all find out the rules for holding meetings and writing a constitution!

NARRATOR'S NOTES - some weeks later:

The club takes shape:

Being in charge of a group of young people more or less her own age, has given Bee confidence. Together they've tackled some difficult problems and go from strength to strength.

Mind you, they've had luck in finding premises. Some clubs struggle on with far less e.g. storing costumes and props in each others' wardrobes - rehearsing in different rooms every week and so on and on. Nevertheless, this doesn't take away from The Group's initiative and drive.

They've now cleared out Mark's Dad's Hut, have met several times in Auntie's Shed, made money from a coffee morning, held a barbecue in Bee's garden, a concert in Mark's Dad's Hut - in order not to pay rent - hilarious performance in which they all directed their own 'bits' while Jane and I froze to death on a chilly bench, a table tennis match in Auntie's Shed for which they charged, according to Bee's Dad, an extortionate fee for entrance. "It *must* be just this once," wailed Auntie.

They got the go-ahead to rent Andrew's brother's Drama Club's Hall (!) complete with *their* awe-inspiring list of 'Musts' and The Group booked it for some time ahead. They'll produce three one-act plays later this season, using as little scenery as possible and either in modern dress or with costumes "we'll throw together".

A meeting is to be held soon in Auntie's Shed to discuss the forming of a 'committee proper'. Bee is not keen to be elected as she feels her first allegiance is to her own club. However, I do hope she at least remains a member of The Group.

POSTSCRIPT

Team:

Dear Bee,

The Group should - as do most clubs - strive for a state of affairs where everyone involved in a production is part of a *team* which itself is an off-shoot of the membership team. Democracy doesn't just happen; a great deal of work must go into bringing about its existence and having achieved that, in holding on to it.

Although some groups, however, wouldn't agree that such over all teamwork is necessary, in my view it's worthwhile keeping your club as a place where everyone 'mucks in', where everyone has equal opportunities - where there are no 'stars' - only experienced players (they'll come) and those who have yet to learn; where all of you have the chance to serve as committee members and fight, if necessary, to bring about any needful changes.

Believe me, clubs like this do exist and so cling to their example like mad and one day, you'll all have memories of a wonderful organisation, that neither time nor distance can sweep away.

XI

PLAY PRODUCTION

SECTION 1

Choosing Plays:

Dear Bee,

So! The Group's first production in the Hall is to be an evening of three one-act plays later in the season. Meantime Pat is so right in suggesting that one of them be presented first at the forth-coming one-act play Festival. A brainwave - for not only will it be fun but an exercise in acting in a theatre plus the bonus of an adjudication. Obviously it also works as a try-out for the Hall production.

That you are to direct the Festival production is great news. So glad you accepted. Discuss with them your lack of know-how and *their's*. You're all in it together.

Considered from your angle it's a god-given chance to share your new-found knowledge on acting; you'll also learn about acting from a director's point of view - a salutary thought.

Reading plays:

May I suggest that you begin by encouraging The Group committee to start reading plays. Insist that they choose three plays not beyond their knowledge of the world (you can consider the wisdom of 'branching out' when they are more experienced) and with a size of cast that whoever is directing can cope with (possibly four - and five at the maximum).

NARRATOR'S NOTES:

We shall have to take all these coming problems one by one; Bee is struggling to find plays for production. The play-reading committee meetings are (wails Bee) "farcical".

Dear Bee,

As you don't need to find suitable plays by tomorrow, try to relax a little over the problem and take it step by step.

Point out to the committee that choosing plays for performance, whether three or one-act plays, is one of the most exacting tasks facing their new drama club.

Because each club has its own methods of deciding on forthcoming productions, I can't give hard and fast rules. Although in time you'll work out your own, clearly, certain factors must come first before you make final choice of plays.

e.g.: how many people are available;

players' suitability for casting;

can your workshop cope with the setting required for a chosen play? And so on...

I have amused myself by imagining a dialogue between the committee members of our fictitious club. As you read it, work out where you agree with what's going on and where you would say "We can do better than that!"

SCENE: *the draughty club room where the committee meet to choose a play for the next production:*

PRESIDENT: *(briskly)* Right! That's that done. What's next?

(She looks at secretary who whispers: "Choice of play".)

PRESIDENT: *(sighing)* Oh dear! Yes! Choice of play.

DIRECTOR: Sorry to interrupt, but you are keeping in mind that I'm not available to direct the next play?

SECRETARY: *(who'd dearly like to keep the director in his place, but will never see the day)* That's all in hand I've written to ---- and she's agreed to take on the next production subject to...

DIRECTOR: *(gloomily)* availability of cast, I suppose.

SECRETARY: Exactly!

(tiny pause)

PRESIDENT: *(hopefully)* Well? No problems? *(She looks enquiringly at secretary.)* What's the response from members?

SECRETARY: *(unhappily)* Same as usual: only a few actually took the trouble to reply.

STAGE DIRECTOR: You knew that would happen! Why didn't you put up a notice in the clubroom, *as I suggested,* and get them to sign it on the spot.

SECRETARY: *(bridling)* It's all very well, but they don't always know at the last play whether they're free for the next and when I ask them, they say they have to check dates and...

DIRECTOR: Nonsense! Really keen players sign straight away...

SECRETARY: Oh, they do that all right - and then tell you later they "can't oblige".

(She glares at the director, who glares back.)

PRESIDENT: *(firmly)* All right. The point is: what do we do now?

COMMITTEE MEMBER: *(pouring oil)* What if we each take on so many members to phone, find out who's available, then talk about it at the next meeting?

(With some relief, the president sees the committee nodding in agreement.)

Interesting? It certainly leaves the question open on how availability of cast is best dealt with. With three plays to cast, deal with it you must and before any other consideration - including choice of play.

Problems to think about:

Do you expect your new members to be interested when they don't as yet know what the plays will be - or should they make themselves available, whatever the plays?

Obviously some of these problems won't arise till you start producing three-act plays in a year or so. Nonetheless, it's not too early for the interim committee to face up to the problems connected with choosing three one-act plays.

As president guide them through the following:

1. Let the committee choose three of their members to find plays and pass those they consider suitable, around full committee. All reading should be finished before the full committee meets again.

2. Know who is willing to direct; it might be possible for you to direct two i.e. including the one for the Festival! Suggest to the committee that they might invite a 'likely one' noted from the concert production - or - how would they feel about asking Simon to direct the third one? This would mean that all The Group would be free to act.

3. Chosen directors should be present at play reading discussions and a) read the plays available and/or b) present their own offerings for discussion and approval.

All of you bear in mind that you'll need variety for an evening of one-act plays e.g. they needn't all be comedy.

(Directors should note that they may have to share some players i.e. some will have to appear in more than one play.)

4. Before making a definite choice of plays, hold a meeting of the club and let them in on what's happening. Inform them that subject to players' availability certain plays will be produced.

Ask them to give a firm commitment that they will be available for the Hall production. Some, of course, will be committed by being in the Festival play to be repeated in the Hall.

5. You do not have a large enough membership to divide into actors and back stage enthusiasts. Ask them all to 'sign up' for backstage work and to write in their preference for e.g. painting scenery, wardrobe, props, front of house work and... you're bound to think up more tasks! In a newly formed club, members should be prepared not only to act but to be stage crew the moment they're off stage.

6. There's no use in choosing a play which requires a good (suitable) lead player if none exists.

N.B. As president make sure that your committee are in agreement about all decisions.

SCENE: *Same old room - next meeting of committee:*

PRESIDENT: *(briskly - she always starts briskly)* Now! Let's hear how we've got on about casting the next play.

SECRETARY: Here's the list - it looks as though we've a good number to call on.

PRESIDENT: *(looking swiftly down the list)* Pass it round, will you? Next question: can we hear about the plays the sub-committee have come up with?

(Ever hopeful, she looks round the committee.)

DIRECTOR: We-e-ll! There's one or two 'possibles' - a 'costume' drama...

TREASURER: *(smugly)* that's out for a start! *(They all glower at her.)* I've warned you often enough that our finances won't run to two expensively dressed plays this season...

DIRECTOR: *(exploding in righteous wrath)* For heaven's sake! When is this club going to spend money on the right things and put together its own wardrobe? *(This is a favourite hobby-horse.)*

PRESIDENT: *(dryly)* Just as soon as we can find an expert team of dress-makers/designers prepared to take on all the work involved.

TREASURER: Not to mention the outlay!

(pause)

PRESIDENT: Any other plays?

DIRECTOR: We read an excellent modern comedy... *(He looks broodingly at the stage director and mutters something.)*

PRESIDENT: Sorry? We didn't catch what you said.

DIRECTOR: *(loudly)* I said - it requires two sets.

STAGE DIR.: *(up in arms)* You can forget that! There's no way...

DIRECTOR: *(fuming)* Really! Why I'm asked to chair a sub-committee...

PRESIDENT: Perhaps we could hear the stage director's reasons for throwing this play out?

(The director leans back and studies the damp patches on the ceiling.)

STAGE DIR.: Right! We don't, unfortunately, have the manpower to see it through, especially as a large cast was mentioned which means that with most members acting, we can't get hold of people either to help with the painting or to work back stage.

DIRECTOR: *(sitting upright)* That all *sounds* reasonable. On the other hand, this committee has got to think seriously about ways of getting round such problems.

PRESIDENT: Perhaps this could appear on the next agenda? In the meantime are there any other plays to consider?

Pay no attention to the fact that the committee argue heatedly; who wants a committee full of yes-men? You'll find that the more affairs are talked about openly at your own play choosing meetings, the more things will get done - eventually.

The dialogue, in any case was not to show you how things must be tackled; merely to point out that often that is how they are tackled.

So? Decide firmly on what you wish the play reading committee to get on with and spell out the requirements and plan of action.

NARRATOR'S NOTES:

...and a good time was had by all! Plays at last chosen. Simon, from her own club, is to direct a drama and Bee, two comedies, including the one she is producing for the Festival.

Simon, who is a little older than any of them and with some acting experience, had originally volunteered to help Bee at rehearsals by taking notes for her. He has got more than he bargained for! The Group seem to like and respect him, while Bee is certainly finding it a relief to share problems with someone.

SECTION 2

The One-Act Play Festival:

During rehearsals I shall write letters to you at three different stages during production. Good luck!

STAGE 1:

Director reads the play.

Dear Bee,

It's time now for you to study your chosen play. As you read, view the play from different aspects:

1. Read it as a story. Imagine yourself in the audience and enjoying the play for the first time.

2. Read it again. Note how the playwright begins the play - giving time for the audience to become acquainted with the characters. Note where the first little twist in the plot starts and how the play builds to a climax.

3. Read it again. See the play 'moving' in your mind as the characters (are they coming alive for you?) journey through the ups and downs of the plot.

4. Are you beginning to see a suitable setting for the players? - visualize first then jot down any tentative ideas for entrances (doors) and space available.

5. Read once again before the casting reading.

Casting reading:

Tell the story of the play to the members and briefly outline the characters. Hand out books and read the play with members taking the different parts. Decide who is to read the various parts and also allow players to choose parts they feel they'd like to try. Sometimes you get a surprise when a player gives a reading you hadn't expected. All the time, you make notes.

These notes may be about their voices (think of contrast between the characters) interpretation, suitability - in age for example - and anything else which interests you e.g. sometimes it's of value to note their height: you don't want to end up with a hero six inches smaller than the heroine. If the play calls for a sylph-like daughter of the house, don't choose a wee plump lassie.

Let the chosen cast know your decision as soon as possible then call a meeting of these so-new young players. A good idea is to let them understand the basic things I told you way back when you played 'Mary'. How about beginning with the term 'Director'?

Talk about the story line and give some idea of how you see the characters. Don't be too specific - you want to see what the cast can bring to their parts.

The week following a successful casting reading:

The director works on play:

Dear Bee,

Once again to the quietness of your own room to read your chosen play!

This time note particularly that in this well-written one-act play (thanks for sending me a copy) the playwright has only a short introduction before he gets right into the story and twists and turns the plot quickly and amusingly (the 'meaty' bits!) before leading into a satisfying outcome - and climax - which will delight the audience.

STAGE LAYOUT:

Now design your set. Decide where the door and the window are to be. Keep the door fairly upstage either on one 'wall' left or right or - in the back 'wall'. Bear in mind that players shouldn't be asked to make important entrances from a door downstage i.e. near the audience. Why? Because they then have to walk away from the audience to reach centre stage. It's far easier for them to walk down to an acting position and it's also important for the audience to get a good look at whoever is coming onstage.

Don't clutter the stage with large furniture e.g. huge sofas. Don't allow furniture to take up the best positions onstage i.e. the centre. (Far too often in one-act play festivals a massive table straddles centre stage while the cast edge in a distraught way around the small area left to them in the corners.)

PLOTTING MOVES:

Concentrate first on the BASICS:

-that the character speaking must always be clearly seen by the audience. Make sure no one is standing between the speaker and the audience (it happens - and it's called 'masking').

-that generally the most effective part of the stage from which to speak i.e. for dialogue essential to the plot, is in the central area. From here, the character important to the scene being played can stand slightly upstage of those s/he is addressing i.e. dominates the scene.

Essential: Give great attention to the ENTRANCES of your cast. Can they be seen? Where are the players on the entrance of another? Have you prepared your groupings on-stage before an entrance so that the newcomer has a place to go!

Give great attention to EXITS. Is the exit important? Does the player have a line to say essential to the plot before going 'off'?:

-if the LINE is important, have the player AT THE DOOR before speaking. The WORDS then hold the attention of audience.

-if the MOVE is important, have the player say the line BEFORE moving to door while the other players are perhaps silent. The EXIT itself holds the attention of the audience.

ALWAYS work out what it is you wish the audience to pay attention to at any given moment. CLARITY of move and lines.

Stay CLEAR of furniture.

Move players only for reasons essential to the action of play: Suppose C is about to divulge earth-shattering news. You must work out the move(s) *prior* to this moment so that C stands in a commanding position to make his announcement.

Every character has his or her own personality - their movement differs - at its simplest, a character may make nervous moves while another requires purposeful moves.

Always keep personality in mind - Moves rehearsal are not really humdrum - people move for psychological reasons as well as wanting to arrive somewhere; in other words HOW do they move and WHY?

Don't worry about the humour of the play at the moment. The players are too concerned with being in the right place at the right time to think of laughs. Humour depends a lot on TIMING and that will come with rehearsal. Just be sure that they're in good positions from which to speak hilarious lines.

Be encouraging. Always tell them when you're pleased.

Meaning of direction:

Dear Bee,

As I said - it may be useful to begin by explaining the meaning of direction and the responsibilities of a director. And too - a word on being part of a team won't go amiss. Let's start with:

THE DIRECTOR:

(The true producer of all the plays presented by The Group is the club itself, which finances the performances, organizes every business detail and is responsible to the membership for everything undertaken in their name.)

The director, however, is in charge only of the current play and is responsible for its presentation. S/he controls the cast and has the last word regarding choice of scenery, properties, furniture, costume and lighting. Although a director's word is law on everything to do with the performance, the stage manager passes on to the backstage team the decrees of the director.

By the way - DRAMA: the term comes from a Greek word meaning Being and Doing - which is a satisfying and satisfactory definition to pass on to your players.

THE CAST:

The actors in a play - it won't do any harm for the cast to think of their part in a production team.

They should strive for a state of affairs where everyone involved in a production feels part of a team (which itself forms an integral part of the membership). They work with - and for - the director. Democracy won't just happen; a great deal of work goes into bringing about its existence and having achieved that, in holding on to it.

A production benefits when backstage and onstage people show equal respect for each other's work. Director and everyone in the production must work hard to achieve a TEAM. All must know what's expected from them.

However, although some groups wouldn't agree that such over all team work is necessary, it's worthwhile to keep your club as a place where everyone 'mucks in', where everyone has equal opportunity, where there are no 'stars' - only experienced players - and those who have yet to learn; where all of you have the chance to serve as committee members and fight, if necessary, to bring in needful changes. Believe me, such clubs do exist and so cling to their example like mad and one day, you'll all have memories that neither time nor distance can sweep away.

First rehearsal:

MOVES: You've worked out at home *why* you want players to move. Obvious reasons may be:

That it's necessary e.g. to get player A from the door to the window because he's supposed to make some comment on what he sees.

That it's now necessary for player B to join him; an appropriate move across stage gives her an arrival point beside A.

These are what I call 'walk-abouts' made in order that players arrive in positions essential to the requirements of the story.

When you are plotting these moves, keep in mind where other characters are when you move either A or B.

What, for instance, happens to C's move after B has gone to the window? You can't move B into a position which will mask C who has a line to say.

Other moves, which I'll call 'emotional' moves, are made for different reasons from above. These have to do with the interpretation of a part e.g. Suppose A has to tell B something which he is afraid to say. In this case, it may be better to give A a slight move *away* from B, before he plucks up courage to turn and say his line.

NARRATOR'S NOTES:

...and she's a bit muddled about "telling them where to stand." (!) I think I'll send her one or two of my little lists!

Instructions on giving moves:

Directions to move left or right or whatever:

Always give these from the actor's point of view as he or she faces the audience. In other words, to someone sitting in the auditorium, the player is moving to the right of the stage while as far as the player is concerned, the move is to the left.

Instruct the cast

Move L. - and the player follows left hand.

Move R. - and the player follows right hand.

Centre stage is just what it says - in the middle.

Left centre - move left of centre.

Right centre - move right of centre.
Down stage - and your player moves to the front of stage.
Down stage Left and Downstage Right - tell your cast in which direction to move off.
Upstage Left and Right - tell the player to move towards the back of the stage in whatever direction called for.
Move upstage of settee would mean - move ABOVE it. You might tell a player to: Move upstage right of settee i.e. walk above and to the right of settee.

Abbreviations:

(You've probably made up your own abbreviations. However, you could let the cast see a list of the following.) N.B. They must see the note on Stage Directions first.

LEFT:	L.	LEFT CENTRE:	L.O.
RIGHT:	R.	RIGHT CENTRE:	R.O.
CENTRE:	O.		
UPSTAGE:	U.S.	UPSTAGE CENTRE:	U.S.O.
DOWNSTAGE:	D.S.	DOWNSTAGE CENTRE:	D.S.O.
CROSS STAGE:	X.	CROSS TO CENTRE:	X.O.
MOVE TO CENTRE LEFT:	M.O.L.		
CROSS DOWNSTAGE RIGHT:	X.D.S.R.		

Number chairs on the stage plan and refer to ch.1, ch.2, ch.3. - Cross below chair 1. to above chair 3 = X bl. ch.1 - ab. ch.3.

Although it's useful to make up your own abbreviations, don't overdo it as you can find yourself in a right old muddle trying to decipher your own cleverness.

Stick to a few well-tried ones and give the cast time to write instructions if they're obviously not coping with shorthand!

Encourage your cast to note (briefly) where their partner is when they themselves start to move. It keeps the picture clear when they're at home going over your instructions on MOVES.

STAGE 2:

Later rehearsals:

BOOKS DOWN:

Dear Bee,

It's 'Books down' period and time for another letter - once the walk-about moves have been thoroughly rehearsed and you're satisfied with them, from then on the cast rely on the prompter to help them with lines.

Keep in mind that one or two of the cast will partly memorise their lines before the others stop clinging to their scripts. When these players ask to 'try without books', let them. Some players benefit from struggling with lines while they're in search of character.

As the rehearsals continue, take note of how the cast attend to your instructions. Be firm! For instance, when a player has received the same instruction three times (it happens) you must show faint? displeasure.

You may find that when the cast are familiar with their moves, they become unhappy about some of them. Although you must always listen to their complaints, should you decide that you are right, try to convince them of this; they must remember that the director is responsible for the whole picture. Don't bully; should their ideas be sound, accept them.

Relationships:

Over the past year we've discussed many aspects of acting. Now's the time to apply some of that advice. With directing, the difference is that you have more than your own character to think about. Your attention is not only on individual personalities, but to a greater extent than before, on the relationships between them.

Make sure that each player's interpretation fits in with the requirements of the play. Here, the same advice applies as for MOVES i.e. listen to their ideas and accept them if good.

Techniques:

Help your players in technique needed for one effect or another. Remember? e.g. pointing lines; learning to listen; the use of pause; variety in pace; building to climaxes; different kinds of entrances and exits and so on.

Don't, however, give them indigestion - a little dose of information at each rehearsal. Whatever the technique, be sure that their character is of the first importance.

Arouse their interest in words, their colour, the hiding of other meaning behind the words used and the emphasis given.

Improvisation:

A twenty minute improvisation period at the start of each rehearsal will pay dividends. Look back at what we said about improvisation.

Run through:

Finally, take a rehearsal complete in every detail. Retire to the back of the shed and nudge Simon when you want a note taken as *you* keep your eyes on the performance. At your magic words "Curtain Up" the cast act as if in front of an audience.

When they forget words, the prompter supplies them; if Props fails to give someone the correct article or the Effects team forget to ring the telephone bell or a player makes a late entrance, on they must go as if for real.

After working on the faulty bits with the cast you again retire and again it's "Curtain Up". And this time there are no mistakes. At least, not the same ones.

Character:

Don't overdo the striving for technical perfection; call a halt at some point and return to concentrating on character.

Atmosphere:

Never allow a cast to leave rehearsal in a depressed mood. However, players often sense when their work is not up to the standard you're looking for and take this thought home to mull over.

NARRATOR'S NOTES:

Director's point of view:

Bee is finding out what an exhausting responsibility it is to direct. That said, there's no doubt that she loves the excitement and exhilaration of it all.

At first she couldn't bring herself to command proceedings and confided: "I could hear me being bossy." She's learning to instruct as "if I'm telling them something they know but have just forgotten for the minute." Over the phone she remarked, "You've maybe never noticed, but actors don't like to think anyone is helping - I mean - they'd rather believe it's 'all my own work'."

I wonder if I've ever noticed.

Dear Bee,

When you played 'Julia' I promised to give you notes on how to 'use' furniture on stage so that it worked for you, rather than against. Here they are now.

Using furniture:

Furniture may be guide and ally as we said; it's unwise, however, for players to use it as a crutch.

Perhaps they've seen plays in which the actors clung on to chairs, tables and the backs of sofas as if they couldn't totter anywhere without support. Don't let them imitate such players. Watch them move around the stage and when they sidle past chairs and tables, remind them to stay just a little away from them.

Although movement on stage certainly looks ugly when players constantly hang on to furniture, make clear it's not just a question of appearance. Impact on audience is their concern and lines spoken while they stand around with hands glued to every available piece of wood, weakens performance. Not only that, but when the time comes to move, players require to straighten and step back before setting off again.

Suggest e.g.: Stay a little above (and a little to the side) of the sofa. They'll discover how much easier it is to move comfortably in any direction needed. It benefits a player to say important lines when not cut in half by furniture.

Say: "To go right - put the weight on your left foot - and set off with your right."
"To go left - place the weight on the right foot and sally forth with the left."

As a good director:

Don't plan vital speeches to be said behind wood.
Don't allow players to cling to any piece of furniture for support - moral or otherwise.

Obviously there will be occasions in the play when the author instructs characters to 'use' furniture e.g. (and let's refer to the 'Julia' play) Julia leans over her father's chair - Simon clutches the back of the sofa - and so on. These notes are necessary to the story line - and indeed, the director may use a few of his own to add variety to the players' moves. It's therefore essential that the cast don't add their own list of leaning, clutching, holding on to, slouching and hiding behind wood!

NARRATOR'S NOTES:

While there is great joy in encouraging full-of-beans, super-charged young players, now and again their unexpected response can leave a director feeling - a trifle worn. (As Bee discovered.)

Ad-libbing:

Dear Bee,

Delighted that the improvisation periods go well. Console yourself with that thought while I explain what may have happened when things got out of hand.

In the first place, it isn't wrong to carry improvisation into the actual play as long as it's confined to work previously accepted AT REHEARSAL by the director. In the second place, no player has the right to alter the lines in a given script; these belong to the playwright. What Mark and Andrew were indulging in is known as ad-libbing i.e. making it up as they went along.

No matter how clever and funny they thought they were being (and encouraged by a highly amused cast) you must, I'm afraid, spell out in clear terms your refusal to accept such goings-on. You could ask them politely whether they were having difficulty in learning the given words and if so, could you offer them extra rehearsal time! But as that's too harsh, simply stop work, sit down and explain to the cast the dangers arising from not sticking to rehearsed lines, movement and stage business.

Better still, ask everybody to think out what these may be. Ad-libbing differs from improvisation as we've talked about it, in that improvisation is acting out scenes as a means of exploring character at rehearsal; ad-libbing is generally used as a despairing remedy in performance when an awful silence falls on stage, the prompter has apparently gone home, your fellow players are struck dumb and you fill the gap by chattering away in your own words.

We mentioned ages ago how a cast may be forced into this situation out of necessity when a player fails to come in on a broken line, or if a player is late on entrance leaving you to die a thousand deaths solo on stage.

It's just as well that you've experienced having to deal with this in directing, for ad-libbing lines or stage business is something to be avoided whenever possible; it's a selfish ploy when it's done with total lack of consideration for other players and without consultation with either their partners or the director - all it shows is a lack of DISCIPLINE!

And when a player is driven to it, it's not a happy ploy as I was reminded not long ago in a delightful tale of woe. Correction: delightful to laugh about after the event...

Playing in pantomime, the actor concerned was changed by a fiendish spell into a cat. For a few moments he enjoyed prowling around the set until it dawned on him (though perhaps it seemed more like a brick hitting him) that his partner was late on entrance.

No longer "particularly enjoying myself" - one of these charming understatements - there was nothing for it but to continue his feline progress.

As the seconds ticked by, his prowling became that of a highly-strung cat; he felt "a little desperate" for, as he added succinctly, "How the hell can you ad-lib when all you've got to say is 'miaow'?"

Next rehearsal, Bee, impress on Andrew and the others that ad-libbing is for use in dire emergencies only. And may they pray that the need to 'make it up' never arises.

Inspiration:

Dear Bee,

You'll often find that whenever players have become used to acting without their scripts at rehearsals, they start 'putting things in'; they experiment with saying lines in different ways and adding gestures and facial responses they hadn't dreamed up before. As director, you must decide whether or not you feel a) that they have added a welcome dimension to their characters and b) that it is of value to the play as a whole. When you've made your decisions, make these known to the players involved.

From what you say, Pat and the others have got a little beyond themselves: they now think they know as much as, if not more than, the director. Be tolerant in the way you treat this - it's natural for actors to try to get into the skin of a character; on the other hand, the play is *your* responsibility and they must follow your instructions.

Pat's dramatic "You don't understand! I felt inspired!" is fine - the trouble is that when actors believe they're inspired, it generally means that they've gone overboard with a life belt, and every one else can sink as far as they're concerned.

NARRATOR'S NOTES:

Sent Bee a word or two on CLARITY. She's at that stage of rehearsal when the thought may come in useful.

Clarity:

A lovely word, Bee - crisp, clear, crystalline! Clarity is the key to all that will happen in your play. As director, you must work out each phase, each action, each climax, each scene with precision. Try first to unearth and follow the playwright's wishes. Think of the variations in rhythm which allow the play to flow lucidly.

Your players must know exactly where each scene leads. (Help them.) Sure then of their moves, they contrast and vary their lines and scenes with CLARITY. Listen to their voices as they express their characters' thoughts in such a way that it seems they come fresh and new from their minds.

Technique? Of course, Legitimate? Yes - when your players act from within the clear framework you have given them that allows them to act with sincerity.

Sincerity, Bee - remember! Whatever the technique, make sure the players are sincere in their characterizations.

NARRATOR'S NOTES:

An urgent call from Bee who's suddenly thought of make-up - fortunately in plenty of time to do something about it.

Make-up:

Dear Bee,

After the festival is over, have a look in the Library for books on the art of make-up. Meantime, here's some suggestions:

Although the best ways to learn how to put on make-up are by watching others (you did that yourself) and by the players trying it out for themselves, for this one-act play you should invite someone knowledgeable in this art (how about Mrs. M.?) to come to Auntie's Shed to advise and demonstrate. She'll probably show you by making-up the cast in the parts they are to play.

As you can't expect her to provide the make-up, club finances will have to stretch to buying a box of greasepaints essential to your production. Mrs. M. can advise here so that you don't waste money on 'fancy' colours!

(Later on, most of the players will probably like to buy at least some of their own.)

Take plenty of removal cream and cotton wool so that the cast can wipe their faces clean at the end of the play. Everyone should have their own towel and soap and if anyone has sensitive skin, lacto-calomine is soothing.

Mundane advice? You'd be surprised just how many players leave essentials at home i.e. if they thought of them in the first place! You'll learn enough to get through this play by following what I've suggested. Later, make-up classes are a MUST.

Greasepaint, incidentally, isn't put on in order to beautify except when the character played is intended to be either a lovely woman or a handsome man.

Further, a mistake often made by women who use make-up in everyday life, is to suppose that they can use street make-up on stage. Unfortunately, they achieve a result they didn't intend. e.g. In real life, a woman may use a lipstick with a blue tinge - and the same with rouge but NOT under stage lighting, which often makes lips look black or purple and the cheek colouring, aging.

Persuade your committee to set up make-up sessions in Auntie's Shed. There's plenty of experienced players in town and I'm sure they'll be pleased to help you.

STAGE 3:

The dress rehearsal:

Dear Bee,

My third letter: The Festival Committee have told you by now the time allowed for rehearsal on stage; other teams will be there, waiting their turn.

Every moment is precious: the set put up, furniture in position, properties on stage, props. table set out in the wings, cast ready and made-up to go on, prompter in corner and the effects team waiting with their box of tricks (door bell etc.). And all this executed smoothly, swiftly, silently.

Preparation:

You will, of course, have rehearsed to within an inch of their lives all the above tasks in Auntie's Shed.

Lighting:

You'll meet the stage management people and the lighting team. You may already have had the opportunity to discuss the lighting you require. If not that, you will have handed in your lighting plot with clear instructions attached, to the Festival Committee. This gives time for their stage manager to prepare his lighting board.

Don't pretend to be an expert. You can't fool them. Tell them, for example, that the play requires daylight lighting with the apparent source of light coming through the window. Or, with artificial lighting, give details of any source of light on stage e.g. is there supposed to be a centre light - does light shine through a door into another room - are there table lamps?

You must present, marked out on a stage plan, the positions of your furniture, entrance, window, placing of lamps and/or where the light switch is situated.

Put a X where stronger light is required for the main acting areas; indicate the kind of atmosphere needed e.g. do you wish the overall lighting to be warm in tone? It's useless trying for too much; all the same, have a clear idea of the general mood of your set. Should a lamp require to be switched off or on during the play, give them the player's cue line to be said as the light goes off - or on. Incidentally, instruct your cast not to hurry putting on and off lights. Warn them to keep a hand on the switch till the lighting crew produce the light required. The switch only *appears* to work: the actual lighting is worked from the lighting bridge. Nothing is more awful (and giggle making) than to see someone enter a room, press the switch, move off and seconds later, light floods the stage - or vice-versa when they switch off.

NARRATOR'S NOTES:

Bee invited me to 'sit-in' on a rehearsal in Auntie's Shed. I thoroughly enjoyed meeting all Bee's new friends. Bee, Pat and Co. (not to mention Simon) are as excited as it's possible to be without their feet actually leaving the ground. Hope Bee is the first to get a grip of terra firma so that she can hold on to the others.

That said - she's developing an awe-inspiring sense of responsibility. She remarked yesterday: "there'll be time to collapse after the performance!" I replied vaguely that I hoped it wouldn't come to that.

I'll send her a down-to-earth description of back-stage. At the moment, The Group's ideas - which they confided to me! - on what to expect in the theatre are 'way-out' so perhaps some notes will help them not fall over things back stage. (I'm becoming as 'nervy' as they are!)

(Notes for The Group)

Back stage and its paraphernalia:

Here you'll find the dressing rooms and all the people who don't appear on stage at performance. Try to keep out of their way and they'll do the same for you.

Before we begin our journey, let me say that this is a world like no other world and apart from the stage itself the most exciting part of the theatre.

When you are on the empty stage, you'll notice that you're standing within a 'picture' frame - called: -THE PROSCENIUM ARCH-

On either side of the stage is a large space known as: -WINGS- A long passage stretches behind the stage, where players tiptoe on their way from one wing to the other.

With the play in progress, players tread carefully; although the stage blazes with light, little filters through to back stage. What with one thing and another it's as easy as wink to stumble over something. The noise of someone bumping into a sticking-out bit of scenery is invariably followed by the noise of the stage manager swearing at the luckless player in what he fondly imagines is a stage whisper.

-PROPERTY TABLE- set at one side of the stage, though occasionally, a table is needed in each wing. One of Prop's team stands guard with a clip board of notes ready to give players the articles they require on stage.

-STAGE MANAGERS- Though not exactly permanent fixtures in the theatre, they always look as if they'd grown there.

As Simon is your stage manager, in charge of ALL, he'll stand in the right hand wing of the stage (as you look from the audience) along with one or two of the team; yet another clip-board, bulky with sheets of paper detailing your exits and entrances and cues is peered at under a shaded light. (Note here: During Festivals there is also a stage manager present who oversees all the clubs backstage.)

-EFFECTS LIST- Someone else checks this (though Simon keeps an eye on her.) It's Joan, isn't it? Am glad you've sworn not to giggle!

Anyhow, I know she's practised in Auntie's Shed and is ready to ring telephone bells, cue in a knock on the door, signal that it's time for thunder, or wind or crashing glass or horses' hooves or grandfather clocks or a car arriving at the door, or footsteps on the gravel or opening bars of music - whew! - the list is endless, though fortunately for Joan not all are required in *your* play - it may just seem like it.

The paraphernalia for effects is around and about the stage crew; both Simon and Joan keep them within sight and signal for 'action'.

-LIGHTING BRIDGE- You'll see a steel ladder on the wall of one wing which leads up to it. Here someone stands in front of a lighting board with yet another clip-board, to cue in sunshine, drawing room lights, dim a fire or darken a sky or whatever.

-SCENE DOCK- A large area at the back of the stage where scenery is stored.

-FLATS- These are the separate units which make up a scene or a set and are made of canvas framed in wood. The stage crew, with the stage manager in charge and dictating events, stand these upright, side by side. When these are roped together at the back, the impression facing the audience could be e.g. a forest glade or the walls of a sitting room - depending entirely, of course, on how they've been painted.

In your play, the scene is a living room and although Andrew has been in charge of "the painting like mad in the workshop" you've only two flats - one for the window and the other for the door. The theatre stage crew will help at the Festival by lowering stage curtains (roped above the stage) to simulate walls which you must treat as real.

Remember? No box sets made up entirely of flats at a festival. One reason is that they take too long either to put up or dismantle. Another reason is that the custom allows financially embarrassed (!) clubs to enter on an equal level with the more wealthy. Don't rest too easy about that - it's amazing what ingenuity and imagination can do to transform simple sets into joyful masterpieces.

-FLIES- This is the part of the stage above your heads. All sorts of things are stored up here.

-FRONT TABS- Tabs refer to the stage curtains, and front tab refers to the curtain which divides the stage from the auditorium.

-HOUSE- or auditorium. People who work in the coffee room, sell tickets and so on are called Front of House staff. (Most important jobs when you come to work in your own premises.)

-HOUSE LIGHTS- The lights in the auditorium which are controlled from back stage, generally through the stage manager's instructions to the lighting crew. You will hear the stage manager say perhaps: "O.K. ring 'close of Interval' bell." When the bell rings, the audience gulp down their coffee and go back to their seats in time for the next act.

Just before the play re-starts, the stage manager, having checked with front of house manager (generally via inter-com) that everyone is settled, then says, "Dim house lights". Slowly and gradually the house darkens, the restless audience quieten and - "Curtain Up!" whispers the stage manager. Immediately the curtains slowly swish back and we are once again in the world of the play. Another magical moment.

Clearing the stage:

A time limit is set for clearing the stage when the play is over. Either let your stage crew deal with this, or to hurry things on, tell the cast to take off small articles such as cushions, books, ornaments. Whatever way you do it, be sure it's all *rehearsed.*

Better to spend quite a long time on these tasks in the shed rather than swamping your cast with instructions in the theatre, either before performance or at the theatre dress rehearsal. In the theatre, just speak simply to the players, see that everyone is happy - then leave them alone.

Superstition:

Dear Bee,

Haven't a clue for a Festival mascot although a toy busy bee might be the answer - as a personal charm! Where a club mascot is concerned, I've no doubt The Group will dream up something.

As you say, people who work in theatre are often superstitious - though don't expect them to admit to it. Perhaps most people whose work depends for success on a great many unknown factors, don't care to do or say anything which could 'rock the boat'.

I'm not at all superstitious, although I was very fond of our club mascot - a little bear called Davie - dear me! - I do hope they haven't lost him... it's so... Theatre folk, incidentally, don't care for the word 'luck' - it's considered 'unlucky'. Before going on stage they might wish each other "All the best", but never "Good luck".

Don't whistle in the dressing-room - it'll bring forth cries of outrage and you'll be sent outside to turn round three times before being allowed back in.

Mascots from all the clubs litter the dressing rooms - and heaven help the member of a club who has forgotten to bring their good luck charm or whatever.

And now, may I wish you and Simon and the cast all the very best for next week's performance.

P.S. There must be many superstitions connected with theatre. I'm glad I don't know them.

Adjudication:

After their performance, the cast are allowed into the theatre to see another play. When the last play is finished the adjudicator will discuss each of the night's productions in detail: choice of play, setting, costume, make-up and lighting.

The adjudicator is lenient with beginners. This *doesn't* mean you can get away with sloppy instructions to the Festival stage team; they won't take the blame when any mistake is yours.

The acting is considered and the direction. Later, you listen to a private adjudication when you and the cast may ask questions.

On the final night of the Festival, the adjudicator places the teams in order of merit and sums up the week's performances.

N.B. As you're going to repeat this play in the Hall, pay attention to advice given. You can ignore it if you feel you know better!

Festivals in general:

Festivals allow clubs an opportunity to take part in a one-act play (an art form in itself) meet other people and enjoy the atmosphere of theatre. Don't be like some teams and worry so much about your placing that you allow the festive spirit to escape you.

A bonus is the chance to see all the other plays presented. What's the point of winning if you haven't seen the play you beat and learn why the adjudicator placed you first? And vice-versa if you lose.

A week or two after the Festival you receive a written report on your production. Study it and consider the points raised.

NARRATOR'S NOTES:

These 'Festival' letters to Bee are really 'emergency' notes. In a club which trains its own directors, Bee could practise direction within the haven of her own club room. (There'll be time for that in the future.)

After the festival:

Dear Bee,

Thoroughly enjoyed the Festival plays. Though not all offerings were of a high standard - does it matter? - everyone did their best, and that's what festivals are about.

Four plays in the Beginners' section with The Group placed second - you must be proud of them. And too, the adjudicator's comments were of interest:

- the need for players to project more;
- the whole play full of life and enthusiasm (which obviously delighted him;)
- the good use of an excellent set
- while Pat and James received praise for acting, which they deserved.

The adjudicator was encouraging about your direction: and while he pointed out minor weaknesses e.g. in positioning, at the same time he liked the way in which you: handled exits and entrances and achieved variety in pace.

XII

PRACTICE IN DIRECTING

Provision for:

Dear Bee,

To answer your question on clubs encouraging members who want to direct: although some do give opportunities to their players, some find it difficult to find anyone who wishes to do so (!) and those who *have* experienced directors to call on won't risk handing a play over to a novice.

Determined players often gain experience by directing for other clubs who yell for help. In this way they find lots of new friends, work without critics breathing down their necks, make mistakes and discover alone how to put them right.

All great fun - but there are ways in which novice directors may learn without making anyone suffer from their inexperience. A vast increase in the number of amateur directors available might come about if all clubs followed such methods. It's always puzzled me that in the amateur world, far less thought is given to quality of direction than quality of acting. Good acting may stand out in a poorly directed production but that's *not* why people go to the theatre. They go to enjoy a good play, well acted and (although audiences rarely think about direction) well put together.

Methods:

Your comment that: "I'd love to learn more about direction by being an assistant to an experienced director" is a method sometimes used in clubs. It depends of course, on how much the 'experienced one' allows the beginner opportunities to learn - often it's a question of TIME.

As you've seen for yourself recently, there's a lot of talent around: The Group probably contains people who'll turn into good directors, given the chance. A workable method is for them to get together in small groups and produce scenes to perform in front of other members in the Shed. This could prove successful, especially if you invite some experienced directors along to see their productions and at a post-mortem make observations and question the cast and director. There's no doubt that in the free-for-all, knowledge would be passed on. A small step forward would allow the most promising of these budding directors to enter - yes! - a one-act play festival.

Some time ago I came across a scheme which not only benefited the members of a go-ahead club but those invited in to take part. Their committee asked an experienced director from another club to see a performance of their current play and in the week following to give a private adjudication.

This meeting did have an effect. Spirited discussion took place with members and adjudicator exchanging ideas. Most players found they enjoyed responding to criticisms (and praise) from someone not of the home team. Whatever way the arguments turned, everyone hugely relished the opportunity to air their views. The benefit to the guest, apart from the fun of the meeting, was experience in the skill of adjudication!

A good idea is to find out if there are any Directors' Workshops The Group could attend. If not - explore the possibility of local clubs getting together to bring one into being. Another way is to ask an experienced amateur director to take workshops on your own home ground. Summing up I would say that if you *really* want to learn, you'll find a way. Just takes dedication!

NARRATOR'S NOTES:

Bee, fully recovered from all her hard work at the Festival, has started to think about the productions in the Hall. As a budding director she asked me the other day whether what I said about directing was the *only* way to do it! Apparently Simon told her he'd once been in a play where "the director let us please ourselves about where we moved". That I'd have to see!!!

Different approaches to direction:

Dear Bee,

As Simon is directing one of the forthcoming plays what I have to say may be of - er - interest to him.

Looking back to your own experiences, you could say that introducing improvisation into rehearsal was a slightly different way of handling direction. Certainly in improvised acting, players move and speak much as the spirit takes them with the director simply offering guide lines on what is to be attempted in any given scene.

As for the plays to be directed - in which ever which way - the 'good old well-made plays' fit their description exactly, and when produced, the director follows the general instructions of the playwright. For instance, if the author requires the criminal to pop out of a cupboard, this is more likely to satisfy the needs of the play than for Simon to "please himself" by clambering in through the window.

However, where all plays are concerned, imaginative approaches to directing and acting add sparkle. (N.B. while still remaining faithful to the spirit of the written play.) If directors can't bring themselves to do that, they should have chosen another play.

Before we return to directing, let's think about *what's* being directed i.e. THE PLAYS! For instance, I admire those clubs which keep space (however tiny) on their year's timetable which caters for minority audiences (are they *really* in the minority?) who appreciate something other than the all too often 'commercial' offerings of many amateur clubs.

Such plays, presented in the club room to an invited audience, not only give new directors an opportunity to shine, but seasoned directors a chance to branch out. They allow beginners to experiment with bigger parts than they have enjoyed and spiced with improvisation at rehearsal, these add flavour to a year's programme.

It seems to me, that both you and Simon would have enough to inspire you by experimenting with such plays in Auntie's Shed i.e. if she lets you! I'd wager that even then you'd remain 'old-fashioned' enough to instruct your casts to do this, that and t'other and *stick* to it.

Look at it this way: if you'd spent hours working on interpretation, character building and giving lead players, key positions, I doubt (don't you?) that you'd be overjoyed by players wandering hither and thither as the mood took them!

That being said, it's true that amateurs are bound by many unwritten rules which directors and cast have become conditioned to accept as the right - and *only* - way to take rehearsals. For example: Moves rehearsal followed by rehearsals smoothing the moves, followed by scene rehearsals - and on it goes in a well-established pattern.

Not that these patterns are wrong. Far from it. All the same, Simon is right in saying that there are other ways to direct a play and to receive direction. He isn't right in thinking actors do 'their own thing' - unless, of course, the play is a total improvisation on a theme.

SMALL GROUPS: Experimenting with moves and groupings can add variety to rehearsals. When, for example, you or Simon are directing a scene in which only three major characters appear, you can call the actors to private rehearsal and try things out. Undoubtedly, experienced lead players working with an equally experienced director can together, bring an indefinable something to the play. In this kind of atmosphere, players move around, feeling their way into positions, into groups, each finding within the character a *need* to do something or be somewhere. At the same time, each is conscious of the other two players as they achieve groupings which have nothing to do with being given a spot to stand on.

When all's said, groupings are not simply attractive patterns on a stage; a player's performance may improve a hundred per cent when he or she is in a position which feels 'right' not only for the character, but in relation to the others in the scene. At such rehearsals, directors can rely on the intuition of players to work with them for the play and each other - and are invaluable.

Note the emphasis on experience. Some day, you will both achieve joy through directing in this way; meantime, may I suggest - mildly - that you learn the trade by sticking to a few 'rules' before you abandon them for 'higher' things?

NARRATOR'S NOTES:

If I had a wish granted it would be to direct a play of my choice with a very small cast; one where we could explore interpretation and experiment with moves and positions. From minute beginnings, together, in quiet atmosphere, bring about - something wonderful...

The truth is, I suppose, that Bee, Simon and I share dreams about life in theatre...

NARRATOR'S NOTES:

The Group's production - a few weeks later:

Bee is taking a rest after her efforts at the Festival and in the first production at the Hall.

She enjoyed the experience of helping put on three one-act plays. Apparently she and Simon involved themselves in everything going on: scene shifting, make-up, serving coffee at the interval and Bee even prompted her own production while Simon agonised over her lighting cues...

What it is to be energetic! Don't know how they managed to be in several places at once, though I've no doubt at all that Pat and Co. were right with them.

The audience hugely enjoyed themselves, though dare I say sometimes at the wrong moments? I've sworn not to tell Bee, but Jane gave in to muffled squeaks when Andrew came on stage wearing a pullover inside out with the label sticking up. However, I don't suppose he repeated the mistake on the second night; it's hard indeed that in amateur drama one not only has to learn from mistakes but so often in public.

Time to think:

Meantime, Bee says she wants to go on learning about direction and could I think of aspects that she and Simon could work on together. Apparently they've discussed players 'living the part' and wondered if they were on the right lines.

Living the part:

Dear Bee,

Like most aspects this one can be considered from both the director's point of view and that of the player. (You're in a position now to try both!) 'Living the part' is a phrase often heard in drama circles; different people talk about it in different ways.

Think for instance about AUTHORS: Their characters are real to them. Probably they thought about them for a long time while writing the play. Once a play is published, it's likely that what happens to the characters is largely out of their hands. (We're not speaking here about those playwrights who 'sit in' on professional rehearsals to give advice on character.) By the time amateurs are allowed to produce such plays, directors must rely on their own judgment and sensitivity in order to keep faith with the writers. I suppose living writers pray from afar that their creations will come to life in the way they intended.

So - there's one ploy you and Simon could work on. That is, read as many plays as you can, and using your imagination try to 'see' the characters, to sense what makes them 'tick' as you believe the author intended that they should. What then could you do to communicate this, either through acting the part, or directing an entire cast?

This is a difficult task and you won't know whether or not you've succeeded. Only an audience could tell you. On the other hand, reading and interpreting character for one's own gut feelings are essential ways-in to the inner life of an author's creations.

NARRATOR'S NOTES:

Bee is intrigued; she wrote to ask whether it's wrong to see a part in a way perhaps not intended by the writer. There's so many answers to that question, and one of Bee's future satisfactions will be discovering them herself.

Dear Bee,

Be faithful to the author in acting a part and in studying it for production. Try to understand the character 'inside and out' always taking into account other characters' relationships to this person.

However, it's unlikely that playwrights are disappointed when players and directors contribute something to the play they themselves were unaware of - at least consciously - when writing.

Obviously the 'something' brought must be a totally believable aspect of the character's personality as originally created - which brings us to the subject of how THE PLAYER views offering 'something' to the part, which, in a way, is living the part; the character becomes so real to the player that s/he is seen as 'whole' - alive - real.

NARRATOR'S NOTES:

Simon wants to know: "Suppose you see Shakespeare's 'Hamlet' one week and you think Hamlet himself is terrific. The following week you see another actor playing the part quite differently and you think *he's* terrific? Who's to say who's right?

Once again: !!!

Dear Bee,

Where do you and Simon *get* all these questions?

I shan't attempt to answer in full because it brings in so many aspects e.g. you are forgetting that actors' interpretations must fit in with their director's view of the WHOLE PLAY.

Meantime, consider: No two players, given equal talent and perception, see a role in exactly the same way; it is as though the character were sifted through their own personality. How far do you agree with that? Don't tell me! Just work on it!

By the way, don't leave out the question of AUDIENCE in your deliberations on 'living the part'.

When members of an audience mingle in the foyer before going home, you'll often hear: "Wasn't so-and-so marvellous; s/he absolutely lived the part." Not so good, of course, is: "I don't think so-and-so was on form tonight; s/he didn't really live the part."

In the first instance, they mean that the player made them believe in the character and for the duration of the play *was* the character; in the second, they mean that they weren't able to forget the actor and so they couldn't believe in the character.

Their comments aren't intended literally, for no-one can become another. If this were possible, as I've remarked elsewhere (I see no reason why I shouldn't say things again if I want certain points to sink in!) Othello would require a supply of Desdemonas if he insisted on killing one off at every performance.

FINAL LETTER

Dear Bee,

Such fun to write these letters and to share with you these two seasons in drama work; in an odd way it's as though I counsel myself when young!

Meantime, however, we must call a halt. From now on, when either studying a part or directing a play, you may, or may not, apply the advice offered. The point is, that you now have CHOICE. Choice to decide for yourself, between precepts which are of use now and in the future - and those which you will come to recognize as 'not wanted on board' in your satisfying struggles to achieve personal ways-in to acting and directing.

In your chosen hobby - or way of life! - I wish you many happy years of club membership, good comradeship and the choice of drama pursuits which may not only please, but challenge the best in you.

Finally, though there is nothing final about art, I offer some farewell precepts.

NEVER: become self-satisfied with either your acting or directing.

NEVER: divorce yourself from those jobs essential to a successful club: work back-stage, front-of-house, on committee and of course - learn how to prompt! In these ways you will achieve an all-round education in theatre commitment.

NEVER: ignore beginners; encourage and help them. Keep in mind your own experiences.

NEVER: forget that you are a member of a TEAM - no more, no less.

ALWAYS: continue to learn from those you meet; fellow players, cast, directors, stage managers, audience...

ALWAYS: take an interest in plays: in professional theatre, television - and in performances of other clubs' productions. Support each other.

ALWAYS: keep a sense of perspective: there's a world outside drama and it waits to be explored - through participation, reading, travel and observation. Scaling the heights of acting requires that you first climb the rocks of adventurous human living.

ALWAYS: remember the 3Ds of drama - dedication, discipline and damned hard work.

AND ALWAYS ENJOY your chosen activity.

EPILOGUE

As the narrator, meantime, has closed her notebook on Bee's adventures into amateur drama, she feels that this extract from her personal diary may allow readers a more informal - and last - glimpse of Bee and her friends:

It's almost two years since Bee wrote to ask for advice on joining a drama club. So much happened to her in the months following: as far as drama is concerned, she appeared in two 3-act plays, helped set up a new drama club, directed a Festival play, and with Simon, directed a three play programme for The Group.

It's my view - and her mother's - that she should now enjoy a break from it all. Somehow we don't think this is on the cards. Bee, Mrs. M. and Simon have been cast in their club's next production of a serious play - which contains wonderful parts for the three of them. I realize that such a challenge is impossible for Bee to let pass - and I don't blame her one bit! (Her mother and I already look forward to seeing her in a major role!)

Last Saturday was her twenty-first birthday. As it is in the same month in which The Group came in to being, Bee decided to combine her own party with a celebration 'do' for them.

At first this splendid occasion was to take place in Auntie's Shed. For one reason and another, this didn't come about - Auntie herself nearly fainted at the idea, bemoaning the day when her late husband had built "such a monstrous size of a garden shed" - and so Bee, reluctantly, and her mother, delightedly, decided to hold a barbecue and house party in their own home. "In any case," Jane said, "how would we have coped with all the food and - and - so on!"

My invitation said five o'clock, although having been coaxed into lending a hand, I arrived early. Bee, her brothers and Simon dashed in and out of the house and garden seeing to the barbecue and hiding treasure hunt clues in the fruit trees. (Auntie was happily installed in the hammock with "a large lemonade," said Jane's husband blandly.)

Soon the guests arrived, first in ones and twos and then - suddenly - the house and garden were crowded with people. Laughter filled the air, while Jane's two spaniels added to the din by barking hysterically as they rushed from group to group.

Meantime, Simon and Bee, excited and happy, dashed about with the dogs following, as they coaxed the guests to join in the treasure hunt, to eat sausages... James appeared with a guitar and in no time at all, a little cluster from The Group crowded round him in the garden as they roared out one song after another.

Mrs. M. and her husband stuck it out for a while, then quietly slipped in to the house to join some of the "more sensible" folk present. Soon another party had set up in opposition as Mrs. M. at the piano, led the singing of (unashamedly) sentimental ballads.

Jane, worried about the dogs, decided to take them for a walk and I joined her. No need for coats on such a lovely warm evening and we walked down the path in sunshine with the spaniels leaping and bounding joyously at our heels. At the gate Jane stopped to put them on their leads and I looked back.

The garden, bathed in sunlight, was the setting for a play. In the background the small trees and there, stage right, Auntie swinging gently in the hammock; downstage left the guitar player with the cast seated round him - I could see Pat's red curls burning in the light. Centre stage, Simon and Bee cooking sausages - the set spilled over with a riot of colour as the brightness of the girls' frocks mingled with the colours of the flowers and merged into the dappled green backcloth. Sound rose and fell as piano, guitar, ballads and music-hall ditties vied for precedence - thankfully muted from this distance.

Jane sniffed the air. "Burnt sausages and roses!" she said. We laughed and shut the gate.

As we strolled down the quiet road, my thoughts - and I suspect, Jane's too - were in the past: memories crowded in of time gone - other parties, dear friends - another drama club - overlaid with the same kind of laughter and happiness we have left in the garden.

"You're always talking," Jane said, "about the 3Ds of drama - what are they again?"

"Dedication, discipline and damned hard work!"

"Well," she said, "remembering our days, they were certainly present, but drama..."

"Yes, of course," I said, "it's entrancing!"